Glen, Maris Delon
RR 2 Box 423
Monticello, Indiana
, 47960

Glen, Maris Delon
RR 2 Box 423
Monticello, Indiana

Antique and Collectible

Thimbles

and Accessories

by
Averil Mathis

Antique and Collectible

Thimbles

and Accessories

by
Averil Mathis

COLLECTOR BOOKS

A Division of Schroeder Publishing Co., Inc.

The current values in this book should be used only as a guide. They are not intended to set prices, which vary from one section of the country to another. Auction prices as well as dealer prices vary greatly and are affected by condition as well as demand. Neither the Author nor the Publisher assumes responsibility for any losses that might be incurred as a result of consulting this guide.

Additional copies of this book may be ordered from:

Collector Books
P.O. Box 3009
Paducah, KY 42001

@$19.95 Add $1.00 for postage and handling.

Copyright: Averil Mathis, 1986

This book or any part thereof may not be reproduced without the written consent of the Author and Publisher.

To Noal

Acknowledgements

I wish to thank all the dealers, collectors and friends for advice, suggestions and information while assembling my collection. This knowledge has been a great help in compiling this work.

There were those who graciously consented to let me use their catalog pages and/or copy. To these I am grateful: *The Antique Trader Weekly*, Dubuque, Iowa; Dave & Eleanor Brand, Metalsmiths, Dayton, Ohio; The Franklin Mint, Franklin Center, Pennsylvania; P.J.W. Thimbles, Germany; Simons Bros. Co., Philadelphia, Pennsylvania; and John von Hoelle, Author, Wilmington, Delaware.

I am especially indebted to those friends who allowed me the privilege of photographing their collections. It helped provide a much broader view into the world of thimble collecting.

To my husband, Noal, goes my lasting gratitude. He has advised and supported me from the beginning of my thimble collection through my compiling this manuscript.

My thanks goes to the following people who gave me special help:

Kermit Albin	Vernabelle Fritz
Kay Aldridge	Imogene Harbison
Peggy Carroll	R.N. Mathis
J.W. Courter	M.J. Schmidt

Introduction

Collecting thimbles can be rewarding in many ways. The artwork and detail on a thimble is fascinating, almost a miniature picture. There are thimbles for work, for show and for keepsakes, made from a myriad of substances.

This sewing aid has always been a treasured possession of the needleworker. It was a gift one could give without the dangers of social impropriety. At a time most sewing was done by hand, the degree of artwork displayed on a lady's thimble was considered a status symbol. For general use around the home a more durable, less decorated thimble might be used.

Gift thimbles were often engraved. Looking at engraved thimbles is looking into a past that will not speak. They are a testimony of a time, an event, a place or a love that was very special but is locked into the very engraving itself. A World's Columbian Exposition 1892 thimble is engraved inside the lip with: H.M. to J.R. Did they attend? Were they lovers? Another is marked: YALE '95. Was this a graduation date? AUNTIE must have been for a very special aunt for it was a thimble of gold. MOM was also on a gold thimble. A silver one engraved with M.P. 12-25-10 was no doubt a Christmas gift. Then there is a gold thimble which bears marks that look like tiny teeth prints. There are stories that tell of holding a gold thimble on one's finger for babies to use as a teething object. Is this gold one a testimony to this story? The thimble is not out of round as would be the case if one had attempted to make it fit a smaller finger.

This intrigue, the beauty and having something old are some of the reasons to collect thimbles. But there are many beautiful thimbles that are new, which may someday be on the top of some thimble collector's want list.

Whether you specialize in collecting one certain type or run the gamut, your thimble collection will be a source of personal pride.

Every effort has been made to correctly identify each article. The trademarks, touch marks and the Hallmarks have all been taken from the articles themselves.

Contents

Thimble Collecting

Whether you collect thimbles as art, or just for pleasure, you will want to know something about them. Once past the design, you will find markings on a thimble which the maker often used to identify his work. Many of these logos are identified in the back of this book.

You will want to catalog your thimble collection and a few suggestions could make this task easier for you. As you acquire new thimbles, jot down information to simplify the cataloging. Record where purchased, from whom, the date and the cost.

As soon as possible apply self-stick labels to the thimble and record the information with corresponding numbers in a notebook or collector's album. You may number the thimbles chronologically or put them into catagories. Descriptive information of an entry may vary some, but the general information will include: 1) Number, 2) Description, 3) Size, 4) Engraving, 5) Manufacturer and date, 6) Marks, 7) Reference, 8) Where purchased, 9) Date purchased, 10) Cost. A sample layout for an album page is shown after the marks section.

The cost figure may also be useful for insurance purposes. Pages listing entry number and cost may be added in the back of the album or use a cost code to be placed with the thimble description. To establish a personal cost code, use two five letter words with no repeat letters and assign a number 1 through 0 to the letters. Example:

$$L \; I \; G \; H \; T \qquad B \; E \; A \; M \; S$$
$$1 \; 2 \; 3 \; 4 \; 5 \qquad 6 \; 7 \; 8 \; 9 \; 0$$

A thimble costing $25.00 would show: ITSS, and known only to you.

A photograph accompanying the description provides instant recognition and sometimes much better detail of the design than looking directly at the thimble. For recent acquisitions you may clip the picture from the catalog from which it was purchased.

Photographing your thimble is not complicated, nor does it require expensive equipment. A single lens reflex camera with a close-up lens set is sufficient. (I use a Vivitar +1, +2, +4 set.) Take the pictures out-of-doors in the shade, preferrably on the north side of the house. Those taken between 10 AM and 3 PM seem to give the best detail. Shoot slightly down on the thimble to capture some of the thimble top. This angle keeps the entire surface in better focus because of the upward slant of the thimble. You may wish to crop the background of the picture before entering it into your scrap book. Try to keep them cropped to a standard size. The use of a tripod with the camera will help insure a uniform size of the image of the thimble in the photograph. The use of a tripod also insures no movement of the camera on slower speed films.

An added feature would be a graphic likeness of the maker's mark. As a primary identification of the thimble, this visible marking enhances the pictorial value of the cataloging. I drew the marks then made photocopies for use with each entry.

Troy weight is used in measuring the content and the weight of the precious metal in thimbles. Total weight of gold and silver thimbles range from 2 to 5 pennyweight. Below is a chart for Troy weight.

Troy Weight
0.0648 gram = 1 grain (gr.)
3.086 grains = 1 karat (K)
24. grains = 1 pennyweight (dwt.)
20 pennyweight or 480. grains = 1 ounce (oz.)
12 ounces or 5,760. grains = 1 pound troy

Thimbles of Gold

Gold thimbles are what dreams are made of. Fortunate indeed was the seamstress who owned a gold thimble. With the recent increase in gold bullion prices, the acquisition of gold thimbles for collectors becomes more of a dream than a reality.

Thimbles of gold seem to be less frequently marked than those of silver. Many have no maker's mark or gold content stamped on the thimble so it becomes a "Buyer Beware" situation. The marks, if any, may be confusing due to the many variables of content, color and specific manufacturer's markings. The complexity can be seen from the following examples.

K following a number - denotes full karat weight.

Diri Gold - 90% copper, 10% gold.

Scandanavian Gold - 90% copper, 10% gold.

Gold Filled (GF) - A layer of at least 10K gold that is bonded to a base metal and represents at least 5% of total thimble weight.

Gold Plated (GP) - Electroplated with a thin layer of gold which wears off quickly.

Gold Wash - A very thin layer of gold applied primarily inside thimbles, thought to enchance saleability.

Oreide - An alloy which only looks like gold.

Pinchbeck—Another alloy with no gold content.

Black Hills Gold—Actually pyrite, not gold.

24K = 100% pure gold
22K = 91.67% gold - 8.33% other metals
14K = 58.33% gold - 41.67% other metals
10K = 41.67% gold - 58.33% other metals

The color may vary as indicated by this chart.

Color	(Grains)		
	Gold	Silver	Copper
Red	456-460	---	24-20
Pale Red	464	---	16
Extra Deep Red	456	12	12
Deep Red	444	24	12
Citron	440	30	10
Yellow	408	72	---
Pale Yellow	384	96	---
Lemon	360	120	---
Green or pale	312	168	---
White	240	240	---

The following individual company markings have been identified.

Simons Bros. Co. used a trefoil to mark gold filled and an "A" above the Simons shield to mark 14K gold. (See page 169.)

H. Muhr's Sons used a psuedo hallmark for gold filled. (See page 168.)

Stern Bros. Co. used two anchors for gold filled. (See page 169.)

Ketcham McDougall used (o·) to mark 10K gold.

1   2   3

1. Sterling/Gold Band; Mark - Anchor; Stern Bros. Co. **2.** Sterling/Gold band; Mark - Simons shield; Simons Bros. Co. **3.** Gold Filled; Mark - Simons shield, trefoil; Simons Bros. Co.

4   5   6

4. Gold Filled; Mark - Double Anchors; Stern Bros. Co. **5.** Gold; Quaker type; Mark - Star; Thomas F. Brogan. **6.** 14K Gold Paneled; Mark - Arrow with C; Carter Gough & Co.

7   8   9

7. Sterling/Gold band; Mark - Simons shield; Simons Bros. Co. **8.** Sterling/Gold band; Mark - Anchor; Stern Bros. Co. **9.** 10K Gold; Mark - KMD; Ketcham McDougall.

10   11   12

10. Gold; Unmarked. **11.** Sterling/Gold/Stones; Mark - 8 pt. star, Twins; J.A. Henckels. **12.** Sterling/Gold/Stones; Mark - 6 pt. star; Lotthammer - Eber.

13   14   15

13. Gold paneled; Unmarked. **14.** 10K Gold; Mark - KMD, o·; Ketcham & McDougall. **15.** Gold scenic; Mark - "Burr" (like a cocklebur); Unidentified.

16   17   18

16. 14K Gold scenic; Mark - 14K; Unknown. **17.** 10K Gold paneled; Mark - KMD, o·; Ketcham & McDougall. **18.** Gold modern; Mark - Simons shield; Simons Bros. Co.

19   20   21

19. Black Hills Gold (over SS); Custom made. **20.** Sterling/Gold band; Mark - none; Unknown. **21.** Sterling/Gold band; Mark - GSC, Anchor; Goldsmith Stern Co.

22   23   24

22. Sterling/Gold band; Mark - Simons shield; Simons Bros. Co. **23.** Sterling/Gold band; Mark - KMD; Ketcham McDougall. **24.** 14K Gold; Mark - 14K, Simons shield; Simons Bros. Co.

25   26   27

25. Gold vintage; Mark - none; Unidentified. 26. 10K Gold; Mark - B N Co., 10K; Baird-North (Jobbers). 27. Gold; Mark - "Burr"; Unidentified.

28   29   30

28. Gold; Mark - none; Unidentified. 29. 10K Gold scenic; Mark - 10K, Simons shield; Simons Bros. Co. 30. Sterling/Gold band; Mark - Simons shield; Simons Bros. Co.

31   32   33

31. Sterling/Gold band; Mark - Simons shield; Simons Bros. Co. **32.** Sterling/Gold band; Mark - Thimble in star; Waite-Thresher. **33.** Gold; Mark - Simons shield; Simons Bros. Co.

34   35   36

34. Sterling/Gold band; Mark - Simons shield; Simons Bros. Co. **35.** Gold Overlay; Mark - Crown, 18, Lion; H. Muhr's Sons. **36.** 10K Gold; Mark - GSC, Anchor, 10K; Goldsmith-Stern Co.

16

37   38   39

37. Gold plated finger guard; Mark - © Carol Bradley, 1975. 38. Gold paneled; Mark - Star; Barker Mfg. Co. 39. Gold, Faceted rim; Mark - Crown; H. Muhr's Sons.

40   41   42

40. Sterling/Gold band; Mark - Simons shield; Simons Bros. Co. 41. Sterling/Gold band; Mark - Anchor; Stern Bros. Co. 42. Cameo brought from Italy after WW II on new Simons 14K Gold thimble. Presented to author by husband on their 40th Wedding Anniversary, 1985.

43   44   45

43. 14K Gold; Mark - 14K, C in arrow; Carter, Gough & Co. **44.** Gold filled; Mark - Double anchors; Stern Bros. Co. **45.** Sterling/Gold band; Mark - Simons shield; Simons Bros. Co.

46   47   48

46. Sterling/Gold band; Mark - GSC, Anchor; Goldsmith-Stern Co. **47.** Gold; Mark - "Burr"; Unidentified. **48.** 10K Gold; Mark - 10K, GSC, Anchor; Goldsmith Stern Co.

49   50   51

49. 10K Gold; Mark - 10K, GSC, anchor; Goldsmith Stern Co. **50.** 10K Gold scenic; Mark - 10K; Unidentified. **51.** 14K Gold; Mark - Simons shield, A, 14K; Simons Bros. Co.

52   53   54

52. 14K Gold; Mark - 14K, Simons shield; Simons Bros. Co. **53.** Gold filled; Mark - Double anchors; Stern Bros. Co. **54.** 14K Gold; Mark - GSC, 14K, Anchor; Goldsmith Stern Co.

55   56   57

55. 10K Gold paneled; Mark - GSC, 10K, Anchor; Goldsmith Stern Co. 56. Gold filled; Mark - Double anchors; Stern Bros. Co. 57. Gold filled; Mark - Double anchors; Stern Bros. Co.

58   59   60

58. Gold; Mark - none; Unidentified. 59. Sterling/Gold band; Mark - GSC, Anchor; Goldsmith Stern Co. 60. Sterling/Gold band; Mark - Anchor; Stern Bros. Co.

61   62   63

61. Sterling/Gold band; Mark - KMD: Ketcham & McDougall. **62.** 10K Gold; Mark - KMD, 10K; Ketcham & McDougall. **63.** 10K Gold; Mark - GSC, 10K; Goldsmith Stern Co.

64   65   66

64. 14K Gold; Mark - 14K, Simons shield; Simons Bros Co. **65.** Gold; Mark - Star; Thomas F. Brogan. **66.** Gold filled; Mark - Double anchors; Stern Bros. Co.

67   68   69

67. Sterling/Gold band; Mark - GSC, Anchor; Goldsmith Stern Co. **68.** Sterling/Gold band; Mark - Simons shield; Simons Bros. Co. **69.** Sterling/Gold band; Mark - Simons shield; Simons Bros. Co.

70   71   72

70. Sterling/Gold band; Mark - SBC, Anchor; Stern Bros. Co. **71.** Sterling/Gold band; Mark - Star; Thomas F. Brogan. **72.** Sterling/Gold band; Mark - Crown; H. Muhr's Sons.

STERLING SILVER THIMBLES

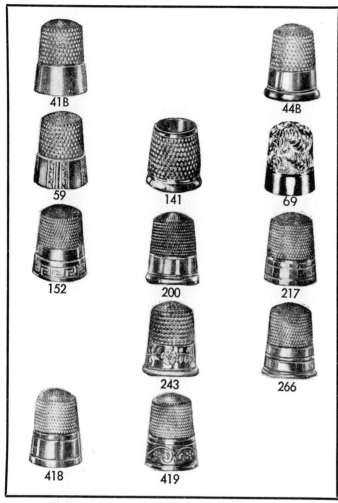

41B

59 141 44B

152 200 69

243 217

418 419 266

200 GOLD FILLED 418 AND 419 GOLD BAND

Catalog pages courtesy of
Simons Bros. Co.
Philadelphia, PA

10 KT. AND 14 KT. GOLD THIMBLES

31AXL 32B 38A 39AB

41AB 69 59

87B 113 152 176

177 209 217 249

424 425 429 148

Thimbles of Silver

Silver is a choice metal for making thimbles. It is malleable, fairly strong, takes a design well and many are engraved for presentation. Considered one of the precious metals, collectors actively seek out exceptional specimens.

The silver content of thimbles referred to as fine or fineness is based on 1000 parts. Some thimbles will carry numbers denoting the fineness as 950, which means 950/1000 parts fine. Silver content on thimbles marked COIN will vary from 850/1000 to 900/1000 reflecting the same silver content of coins of the period in America before 1860. After 1860 most American thimbles were marked STERLING which was the standard for 925/1000 parts fine silver. Aluminum silver, which does contain some silver, is light in weight and takes a very high polish. There are other terms used that are bogus, and the following list should be of some help to determine the content of a thimble.

Mexican Silver - no silver content
Alaska Silver - no silver content
Nickel Silver - no silver content
German Silver - no silver content
Alpaca (or Alpacca) - no silver content
Britannia Silver - .9584 fine silver
Continental Silver - .800 fine silver

Sterling Silver - .925 fine silver
Silver Cased - Electroplated silver
Silver Plated - Electroplated silver
Silver Filled - An article of base metal
   on which is bonded a layer of silver.
Lion Passant - .925 silver (England)
Mercury Head - .925 silver (France)

The cost of collecting silver thimbles rose when the price of silver bullion skyrocketed. Generally the thimble prices have not reflected the decline in silver bullion price. The overall value of the thimble can be based on the condition of the thimble, the complexity of the design, or the rarity of the design or the maker's mark. A current "going price" for silver thimbles can be established by examining and pricing thimbles at flea markets, shops and antique shows. There are some thimbles considered scarce which command premium prices. The bottom line is what you can afford and what that particular thimble means to you or your collection and what you are willing to pay to get it.

Premium Silver Thimbles

A. *Stitch in Time - Saves Nine.*
Sterling thimble marked and made by Simons Bros. Co. A much sought after specimen.

B. *World's Columbian Exposition.*
Exposition buildings in Chicago on the 1492-1892 Exposition site. Simons Bros. Co.

C. *World's Columbian Exposition* 1492-1892. Unmarked, but is credited to Simons Bros. Co. It was sold in the boat holder shown on page 141, No. 723.

D. *Cherubs.* Three cherubs, marked in apex and made by Ketcham & McDougall.

E. *Cherubs.* Cherubs with garlands. Simons Bros. Co. mark in apex and on the band is PAT. NOV 21.05. All thimbles with cherubs are desirable.

F. *Golden Spike*. The official souvenir of the St. Louis, Missouri World's Fair of 1904. The band depicts western expansion and travel showing a train locomotive, which symbolizes the driving of the golden spike joining the Central Pacific and Union Pacific railroads.

G. *Coin or Pure Coin*. These marks were used to denote silver content as used in early American coins. After the STERLING standard was set around 1860, these marks were not used.

H. *The Salem Witch. The Antique Trader Weekly*, October 26, 1983 carried a story, "The Salem Witch". Amni Pear tells us that Daniel Low of Salem, Massachusetts patented the Witch trademark January 19, 1891. This marked the beginning of a huge souvenir trade depicting the Salem Witch, and of these items the thimble is one of the most desirable. Most dealers say there are two of these thimble patterns, but Pear says five distinct patterns have been identified. Ketcham & McDougall and Webster are the best known makers.

The thimble pictured here is a reproduction. It is a Sterling Silver, open top sold by Sylvia Silverman of Brooklyn, New York.

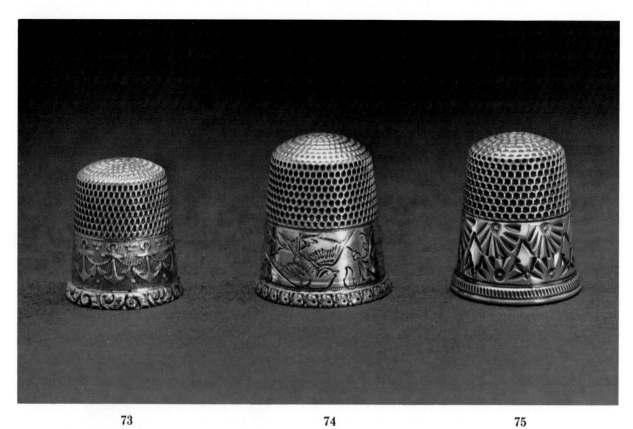

73   74   75

73. SS; Anchors; Mark - Thimble in star; Waite-Thresher. **74.** SS; Birds; Mark - Anchor; Stern Bros. Co.
75. SS; Palmated; Mark - KMD; Ketcham & McDougall.

76   77   78

76. SS; Fleur de Lis; Mark - Star; Thomas F. Brogan. **77.** SS; Floral; Mark - Simons shield; Simons Bros. Co.
78. SS; Floral; Mark - GSC: Goldsmith-Stern Co.

79   80   81

79. SS; Geometric; Mark - Simons shield; Simons Bros. Co. **80.** SS; German; Mark - 8 pt. star; Gabler. **81.** SS; Royal Spa, English; Mark - HG&S, Anchor, Lion, H; Henry Griffith, 1932.

82   83   84

82. SS; Floral; Mark - Simons shield; Simons Bros. Co. **83.** SS; Quaker type; Mark - Simons shield; Simons Bros. Co. **84.** SS; Geometric; Mark - Simons shield; Simons Bros. Co.

85   86   87

85. Silver turtle; Mark - 4 pt. star; Portugal. 86. SS; Scenic; Mark - Simons Shield; Simons Bros. Co. 87. SF; Dorcas; Mark - CH, Dorcas; Charles Horner, England.

88   89   90

88. SS; Oval shields; Mark - Simons shield; Simons Bros. Co. 89. SS; Mark - GSC; Goldsmith-Stern Co. 90. SS; Scenic; Mark - Simons shield; Simons Bros. Co.

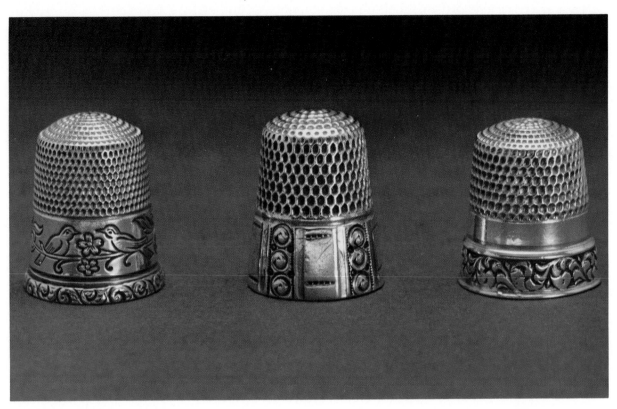

91   92   93

91. SS; Birds; Mark - Simons shield; Simons Bros. Co. **92.** SS; Paneled; Mark - Anchor; Stern Bros. Co. **93.** SS; Feathers; Mark - SBC, Anchor; Stern Bros. Co.

94   95   96

94. SS; Feathers; Mark - Simons shield; Simons Bros. Co. **95.** SS; Floral; Mark - Simons shield; Simons Bros. Co. **96.** SS; Swags; Mark - Anchor; Stern Bros. Co.

97   98   99

97. SS; Floral; Mark - Simons shield; Simons Bros. Co. 98. SS; Fans; Mark - Anchor; Stern Bros. Co. 99. SS; Scenic; Mark - Simons shield; Simons Bros. Co.

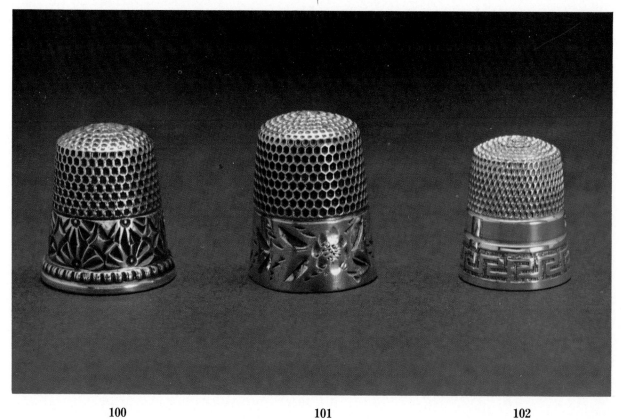

100   101   102

100. SS; Palmated; Mark - KMD; Ketcham & McDougall. 101. SS; Floral; Mark - Simons shield; Simons Bros. Co. 102. SS; Right Greek key; Mark - Simons shield; Simons Bros. Co.

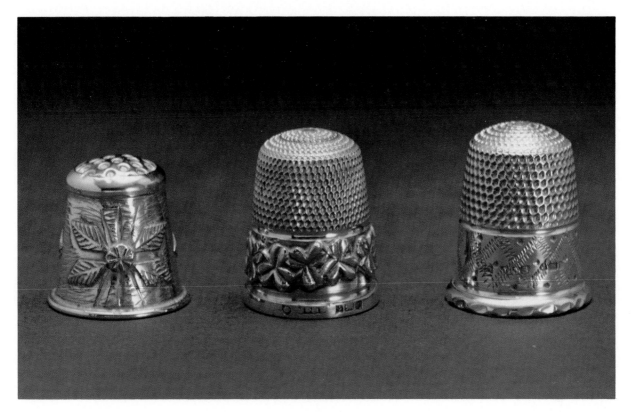

103   104   105

103. Mexico Silver; Mark - Mexico Silver; Mexico. **104.** SS; Mark - JS&S, Anchor, Lion, A; 1975, Birmingham, James Swan and Sons, England. **105.** SS; Mark - JS&S, Flower, Lion, C; 1977, Sheffield, J. Swan & Sons, England.

106   107   108

106. SS; Mark - JS&S, Flower, Lion, D; 1978, Sheffield, Swan & Sons. **107.** SS; Mark - JS&S, Anchor, Lion, Y; 1973, Birmingham, Swan & Sons. **108.** Enamel over SS; Mark - JS&S, Anchor, Lion, C; 1977, Birmingham, James Swan & Sons.

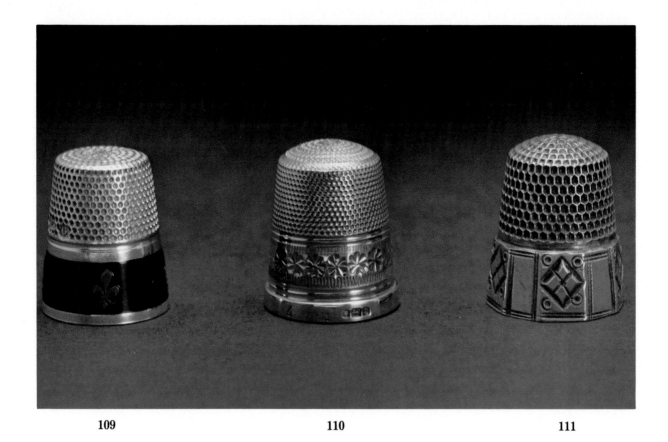

109   110   111

109. SS/Enameled band/Gold inlay design; Mark - 8 pt. star, G, 925; Gabler, Germany. **110.** SS; Mark - JS&S, Flower, Lion, D; 1978, Sheffield, James Swan & Sons, England. **111.** SS; Paneled; Mark - GSC, Anchor; Goldsmith Stern Co.

112   113   114

112. SS; Tai dancers; Mark - Sterling, Siam; Siam. **113.** SS; Palmated border; Mark - JUDD: Unidentified. **114.** SS; Scenic; Mark - illegible; Unidentified.

115   116   117

115. Scenic; Silver?; Mark - none; Mexico. 116. SS; Flowers; Mark - Simons shield; Simons Bros. Co. 117. SS; Flowers; Mark - Thimble in star; Waite-Thresher.

118   119   120

118. SS; Propeller; Mark - Anchor; Stern Bros. Co. 119. SS; Snake & Dot; Mark - Simons shield; Simons Bros. Co. 120. SS; Asters; Mark - Simons shield; Simons Bros. Co.

121   122   123

121. SS; Mini paneled; Mark - Simons shield; Simons Bros. Co. **122.** SS; Mark - KMD; Ketcham & McDougall.
123. SS; Full knurling; Mark - Anchor; Stern Bros. Co.

124   125   126

124. SS; Scenic; Mark - Thimble in star; Waite-Thresher. **125.** 800 Silver; Mark - Star, 209, touchmark, 800; Italy.
126. SF; Dorcas; Mark - CH, Dorcas; Charles Horner, England (note domed top).

127   128   129

127. SS; Mark - Anchor; Stern Bros. Co. **128.** SS; Child's nursery; Mark - Simons shield; Simons Bros. Co.
129. SS; Floral; Mark - KMD; Ketcham & McDougall.

130   131   132

130. SS; Raised circles; Mark - Anchor; Stern Bros. Co. **131.** SS; Tailors thimble; Mark - none; Unidentified.
132. SS; Ocean Wave; Mark - Star; Thomas F. Brogan.

133   134   135

133. SS; Mark - AL&Co., Sterling; Aiken Lambert. **134.** SS; Scenic; Mark - Thimble in star; Waite-Thresher.
135. SS; Scenic; Mark - Star; Thomas F. Brogan.

136   137   138

136. SS; Paneled; Mark - W Co.; Webster Co. **137.** Silver?; Mark - none; Unidentified. **138.** SS; PRISCILLA; Mark
- Pat. May 31. 98, Simons shield, PRISCILLA; Simons Bros. Co.

139　　　　　　　140　　　　　　　141

139. SS; Buildings; Mark - none; Unidentified. **140.** SS; Floral; Mark - Crown; H. Muhr's Sons. **141.** SS; Floral; Mark - Crown; H. Muhr's Sons.

142　　　　　　　143　　　　　　　144

142. SS; Embroidery; Mark - KMD; Ketcham & McDougall. **143.** SS; Louis XV edge; Mark - KMD; Ketcham & McDougall. **144.** SS; Basketweave; Mark - GSC, Anchor; Goldsmith - Stern Co.

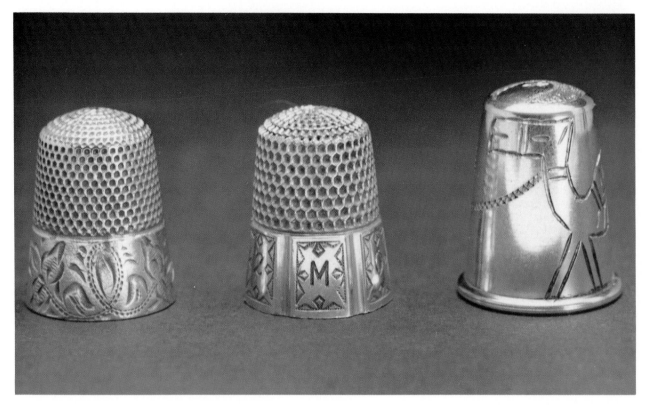

145   146   147

145. SS; Floral; Mark - SBC, Anchor; Stern Bros. Co. **146.** SS; Paneled; Mark - Simons shield; Simons Bros. Co. **147.** SS; Camel; Mark - Jerusalem, Sterling; Jerusalem.

148   149   150

148. Enamel on Sterling; Mark - 6 pt. star; Germany. **149.** SS; "Black Arrow"; Mark - Mercury head, LXF; P. Lenain, France. **150.** SS; "Fleurs et Fruits"; Mark - Mercury head, LXF; P. Lenain, France.

151 152 153

151. SS; Dogwood; Mark - W Co.; Webster Co. **152.** SS; Thistle; Mark - 5 pt. star, 925; Portugal. **153.** SS; Cherubs; Mark - PAT. Nov 21.05, Simons shield; Simons Bros. Co.

154 155 156

154. SS; Feather scroll; Mark - Anchor; Stern Bros. Co. **155.** SS; Paneled; Mark - W. Co.; Webster Co. **156.** SS; Paneled; Mark - Simons shield; Simons Bros. Co.

40

157   158   159

157. Enamel on Sterling; Bicentennial; Mark - Holland. **158.** Enamel on Sterling/Stone cap; Mark - Sterling, Germany. **159.** SS/Enamel band/Stone cap; Mark - Germany, 925; Germany.

160   161   162

160. SS; Applied wire; Mark - Jerusalem, Sterling; Jerusalem. **161.** SS; Wild Rose Bough; Mark - Mercury head, LXF; P. Lenain. **162.** SS; Dance of Graces; Mark - Mercury head, LXF; P. Lenain.

163   164   165

163. SS; Snail & Dot; Mark - Simons shield; Simons Bros. Co. **164.** SS; Tiered; Mark - Crown; H. Muhr's Sons. **165.** SS Ocean wave; Mark - P (Old English); Made by Waite-Thresher for D.C. Percival.

166   167   168

166. SS; Mark - Simons shield; Simons Bros. Co. **167.** SS; Vintage; Mark - GSC, Anchor; Goldsmith-Stern Co. **168.** SS; Garland; Mark - Simons shield; Simons Bros. Co. (Same design as #24 in Gold section)

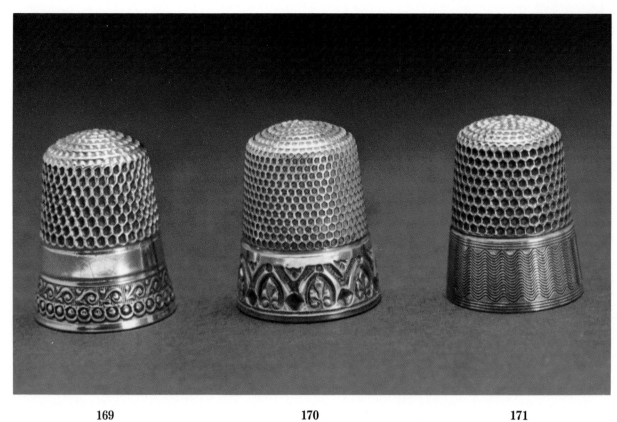

169   170   171

169. SS; Double design; Mark - Anchor; Stern Bros. Co. **170.** SS; Fleur de Lis in arches; Mark - Simons shield, Simons Bros. Co. **171.** SS; Waves; Mark - Thimble in star; Waite-Thresher.

172   173   174

172. SS; Waves; Mark - GSC, Anchor; Goldsmith - Stern Co. **173.** SS; Feather Scroll; Mark - Simons shield; Simons Bros Co. **174.** SS; Mark - Simons shield; Simons Bros. Co.

175   176   177

175. SS; Faceted rim; Mark - KMD; Ketcham & McDougall. **176.** SS; Mark - S; Shepard. **177.** Silver filled; Mark - HG&S, Dreema, Z1; Henry Griffith & Sons, England (Z1=Netherlands import).

178   179   180

178. SS; Rope; Mark - Crown; H. Muhr's Sons. **179.** SS; Stylized flowers; Mark - Simons shield; Simons Bros. Co. **180.** 833 Silver; Mark - 5 pt. star, Cockerel, Touchmark; Portugal.

181   182   183

181. SS; Diamond Knurling; Mark - W Co.; Webster Co. **182.** SS; "MOTHER"; Mark - Simons shield; Simons Bros. Co. **183.** SS; Target band; Mark - Simons shield; Simons Bros. Co.

184   185   186

184. SS; Mark - Simons shield; Simons Bros. Co. **185.** SS; STITCH IN TIME - SAVES NINE; Mark - Simons shield; Simons Bros. **186.** SS; WORLD'S COLUMBIAN EXPOSITION; unmarked but attributed to Simons Bros. Co.

187   188   190

187. SS; Arches; Mark - Thimble in star; Waite-Thresher. **188.** SS; Scroll; Mark - Star; Thomas F. Brogan. **189.** SS; Mark - BRL, 3 crowns, S, V8, F; Sweden.

190   191   192

190. Silver Filled; DORCAS; Mark - CH DORCAS; Charles Horner, England. **191.** Silver filled; DORCAS: Mark - CH DORCAS; Charles Horner, England. **192.** SS; Mark - CH, Lion, Wheat sheaves, A; 1901 Charles Horner, Chester, England.

46

193   194   195

193. Pure Coin; Mark - Mermod Jaccard, Pure Coin; Mermod - Jaccard. **194.** SS; Mark - SBC, Anchor; Stern Bros. Co. **195.** SS; Greek Key; Mark - Simons shield; Simons Bros. Co.

196   197   198

196. SS; Raised Diamonds; Mark - Anchor; Stern Bros. Co. **197.** SS; Reversed Scroll; Mark - KMD; Ketcham & McDougall. **198.** SS; Lily of Valley; Mark - Mercury head, LXF, France; P. Lenain.

199   200   201

199. SS; Mark - Crown; H. Muhr's Sons. 200. SS; Ocean wave; Mark - Thimble in star; Waite-Thresher. 201. SS(?); Tailors; Mark - none; Unidentified.

202   203   204

202. Silver (?); Applied Wire work; Mark - none; Mexico. 203. SS; Mark - Queen's Head, JS&S, Anchor, Lion, C; (Queen's Head mark used on this commerative thimble.); James Swan & Sons, England. 204. SS; Embroidery; Mark - Simons shield; Simons Bros. Co.

205   206   207

205. Silver Cased; "Dorothy" thimble #1931; Iles, England. **206.** 800 Silver; Mark - 8 pt. star, 800; Lotthammer - Eber. **207.** SS; Bee & Birds & Flowers; Mark - 8 pt. star; Gabler, Germany, (Flower centers are inlayed with gold.)

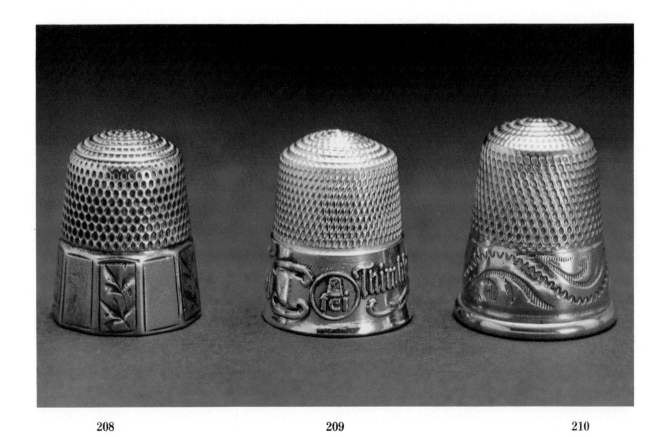

208   209   210

208. SS; Paneled; Mark - Simons shield; Simons Bros. Co. **209.** SS; THIMBLE COLLECTORS INTERNATIONAL; Mark - Simons shield; Simons Bros. Co. (Members Only). **210.** SS; Zipper design; Mark - none (Probably English), Unmarked.

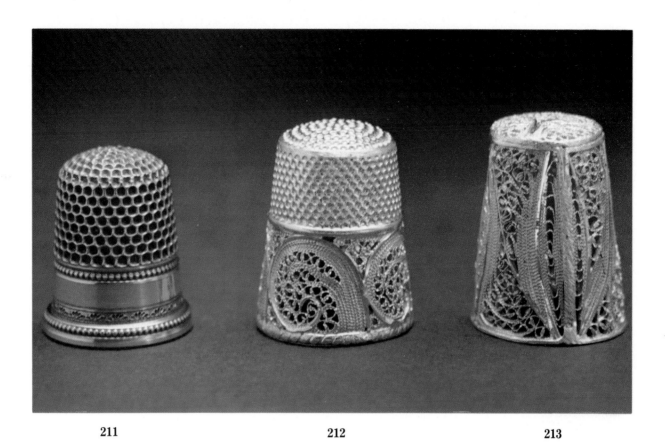

211   212   213

211. SS; Mark - none; Unidentified. 212. SS; Filigree; Mark - none; Portugal. 213. SS; Filigree; Mark - none; Portugal.

214   215   216

214. Silver plated; Mark - 4 pt. star; Portugal. Souvenir of Terceira, an Island in the Azores Chain. 215. SS; Salem Witch, open top; Reproduction by Silverman. 216. SS; Child's thimble; Mark - none; Probably English.

217   218   219

217. SS; Embroidery; Mark - Thimble in star; Waite-Thresher. 218. SS; Mark - Simons shield; Simons Bros. Co. 219. SS; Christmas 1982; Mark - Simons shield; Simons Bros. Co.

220   221   222

220. SS; Mark - SBC, Anchor; Stern Bros. Co. 221. SS; Embossed Roses; Mark - Sterling, UK; Hallmark Cards, Inc. 222. SS; Bees & Flowers; Mark - Anchor; Stern Bros. Co.

223   224   225

223. SS; Diamond Knurling; Mark - KMD; Ketcham & McDougall. **224.** SS; Mark - KMD: Ketcham & McDougall.
225. 800 Silver; Mark - Star, 282, FI, 800; Italy.

226   227   228

226. Enamel over Sterling; Mark - JS&S, Anchor, Lion, G; 1981, James Swan & Son, Birmingham, **England.**
227. SS; Prince Henry; Mark - JS&S, Anchor, Lion, L; 1985, James Swan & Son, Birmingham, England. **228.** SS;
Flowers; Mark - Star; Thomas F. Brogan.

229   239   231

229. SS; Left Greek Key; Mark - GSC, Anchor; Goldsmith - Stern Co. **230.** SS; Feathers; Mark - Anchor; Stern Bros. Co. **231.** SS; Mark - Simons shield; Simons Bros. Co.

232   233   234

232. SS; Buildings; Mark - PAT. SEP 20.81; Unidentified. **233.** SS; Filigree; Mark - Israel. **234.** Enamel over Sterling; Mark - JS&S, Anchor, Lion, H; 1982, James Swan & Son, Birmingham, England.

235   236   237

235. SS; Souvenir; Mark - Simons Shield; Simons Bros. Co. **236.** SS; Prince William; Mark -JS&S, Anchor, Lion, H; 1982, James Swan & Sons, Birmingham, England. **237.** SS; Mark - 925, Sterling, 1136; Towle Silversmiths.

238   239   240

238. SS; Draped Flowers; Mark - Simons shield; Simons Bros. Co. **239.** SS; Diamond Knurling; Mark - KMD; Ketcham & McDougall. **240.** SS; Mark - Sterling, Jerusalem.

241   242   243

241. 800 Silver/Stones; Mark - Star, 209, FI; Italy. **242.** 800 Silver; Mark - 800, star, 209, FI; Italy. **243.** SS; Unicorn; Mark - 6 pt. star, 925, Portugal.

244   245   246

244. SS; Red Riding Hood; Mark - Mercury Head, LXF; P. Lenain, France. **245.** SS; Pierced; Mark - ECB, Sterling; Eleanor Brand. **246.** SS; Pierced; Mark - ECB, Sterling; Eleanor Brand.

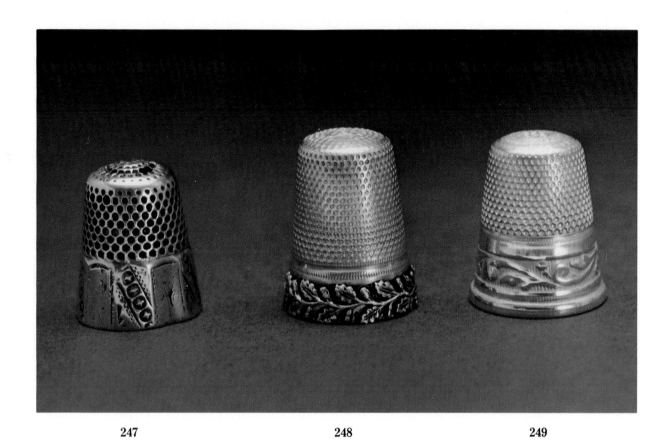

247   248   249

247. SS; Paneled; Mark - Crown; H. Muhr's Sons. **248.** SS; Leaf Border; Mark - 6 pt. star, 925; Germany. **249.** SS; Mark - 8 pt. star; Gabler, Germany.

250   251   252

250. SS; Tailors; Mark - GSC, Anchor; Goldsmith-Stern Co. **251.** Silver Filled; Mark - CH, DORCAS; Charles Horner, England. **252.** SS/Stone top; Mark - 925; Germany.

253   254   255

253. SS; Paneled; Mark - Anchor; Stern Bros. Co. **254.** SS; Buildings; Mark - LAMSON; Unidentified. **255.** SS; Mark - Illegible; Unidentified.

256   257   258

256. SS; Tiered; Mark - JS&S, Anchor, Lion, H; 1982, James Swan & Sons, Birmingham, England. **257.** SS; Beading; Mark - Sterling; Unidentified. **258.** SS; Geometric; Mark - 6 pt. star, 925; Portugal.

259   260   261

259. SS; Tailors; Mark - GSC, Anchor; Goldsmith - Stern Co. **260.** SS; Scrolls; Mark - Star; Thomas F. Brogan.
261. SS; Mark - Crown; H. Muhr's Sons.

262   263   264

262. SS; English Daisies; Mark - JF, Lion, Anchor, M; 1896, James Fenton, Birmingham, England. **263.** SS; Mark
- Anchor; Stern Bros. Co. **264.** SS; Applied Roses; Mark - Thimble in star; Waite-Thresher.

58

265   266   267

265. SS; Paneled; Mark - Simons shield; Simons Bros. Co. **266.** SS; Ovals; Mark - Simons Shield; Simons Bros. Co. **267.** SS; Mark - "Domestic Sewing Machines", Sterling; Unidentified.

268   269   270

268. SS; Geometric; Mark - Simons shield; Simons Bros. Co. **269.** SS; Floral; Mark - Simons shield; Simons Bros. Co. **270.** SS; Geometric; Mark - Star; Thomas F. Brogan.

271   272   273

271. SS; Mark - HG&S, Lion, Wheat sheaves, O; 1898, Chester, H.G. Griffith & Sons, England. **272.** SS; Louis XV edge; Mark - Simons shield; Simons Bros. Co. **273.** SS; Mark - B in Diamond; E. & J. Bass.

274   275   276

274. SS; Scenic; Mark - Crown; H. Muhr's Sons. **275.** SS; Geometric; Mark - Simons shield; Simons Bros. Co. **276.** SS; Mark - "1978 Edition, Limited issue of 5000, Yaacov Yemin, Made in Israel, ST 925."

277   278   279

277. SS; Paneled; Mark - Crown; H. Muhr's Sons. **278.** SS; Mark - Crown; H. Muhr's Sons. **279.** SS; Raised Diamonds; Mark - Anchor, DIAMOND (in apex); Stern Bros. Co.

280   281   282

280. 830 Silver; Mark - 3 Crowns in trefoil, S, 830, S; Sweden. **281.** SS; Beaded; Mark - 8 pt. Star, 925, M; Gabler. **282.** SS; Birds; Mark - Star; Thomas F. Brogan.

283   284   285

283. SS/Stone cap; Mark - Germany, Sterling; Germany. **284.** SS; "JAMES WALKER, THE LONDON JEWELLER"; Mark - JWLtd, Lion, Wheat Sheaves, B, ZI (Netherlands Import); James Walker, Ltd., 1927, Chester, England. **285.** SS; Mark - Simons shield; Simons Bros. Co.

286   287   288

286. SS; Mark - W Co.; Webster Co. **287.** SS; Mark - HG&S, Anchor, Lion, b; Henry Griffith & Sons, 1901, Birmingham, England. **288.** SS; Houses; Mark - Simons shield; Simons Bros. Co.

289   290   291

289. SS; Mt. Vernon; Mark - Sterling; Unidentified. **290.** SS; Mark - S Bros, Lion, Anchor, q; 1890, S. Bros., Birmingham. **291.** SS; Mark - Rd 210800, HW Ltd, Lion, Wheat Sheaves, L; 1894, Chester, HW Ltd, England.

292   293   294

292. SS; Floral; Mark - KMD; Ketcham & McDougall. **293.** SS; Floral; Mark - 8 pt. star; Germany. **294.** SS; Good Luck Symbols; Mark - SBC, Anchor; Stern Bros. Co.

295   296   297

295. SS; Drapes; Mark - 8 pt. Star; Gabler, Germany. **296.** SS; Modern; Mark - SJR, Anchor, Lion, A; 1975, Birmingham, S.J. Rose, England. **297.** SS; Diamond Knurling; Mark - W Co.; Webster Co.

298   299   300

298. SS; Mark - SBC, Anchor; Stern Bros. Co. **299.** SS; Mark - KMD; Ketcham & McDougall. **300.** Silver Cased; Mark - Rd No. 108544; 3 thimbles, Iles, England.

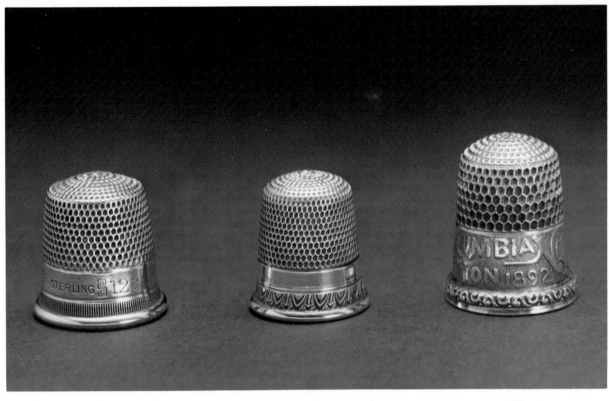

301   302   303

301. SS; Mark - SBC, Anchor; Stern Bros. Co. **302.** SS; Tongue & Dart; Mark - Simons shield; Simons Bros. Co. **303.** SS; World's Columbian Exposition 1492-1892; Simons Bros. Co.

304   305   306

304. SS; "Golden Spike"; Mark - Simons shield; Simons Bros. Co. **305.** SS; Cherubs; Mark - KMD; Ketcham & McDougall. **306.** SS; Scenic; Mark - Simons shield; Simons Bros. Co.

307   308   309

307. SS; Mark - Thimble in Star; Waite-Thresher. 308. SS; Bows; Mark - 6 pt. Star, 2 touchmarks (illegible); Germany. 309. SS; Mark - Star; Thomas F. Brogan.

310   311   312

310. SS; Mark - Simons shield; Simons Bros. Co. 311. SS; Mark - KMD; Ketcham & McDougall. 312. Silver Filled; Mark - PAT. 10 (Early Dorcas); Charles Horner.

313   314   315

313. SS; "THE SPA"; Mark - HG&S, Sterling; Henry Griffith & Sons. **314.** SS; Mark - S; Shepard. **315.** SS; Panel-ed; Mark - Star; Thomas F. Brogan.

316   317   318

316. SS; Scenic; Mark - Thimble in Star; Waite-Thresher. **317.** SS; Mark - SBC, Anchor; Stern Bros. Co. **318.** SS/Stone cap; Mark - Sterling, Germany; German.

319   320   321

319. SS; Scenic; Mark - Anchor; Stern Bros. Co. **320.** SS; Floral; Mark - Thimble in star; **Waite-Thresher.**
321. SS; Vintage; Mark PAT. Jul 9.07, Simons shield; Simons Bros. Co.

322   323   324

322. SS; Cherubs; Mark - PAT. Nov 21.05, Simons shield; Simons Bros. Co. **323.** SS; Paneled; **Mark - Sterling;**
Unidentified. **324.** SS; Mark - Simons shield; Simons Bros. Co.

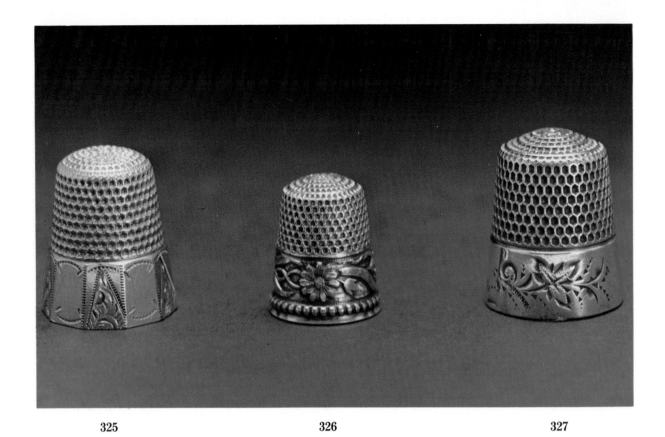

325   326   327

325. SS; Paneled; Mark - Thimble in star; Waite-Thresher. **326.** SS; Flowers; Mark - SBC, Anchor; Stern Bros. Co. **327.** SS; Leaf; Mark - Star; Thomas F. Brogan.

328   329   330

328. SS; Paneled; Mark - SBC, Anchor; Stern Bros. Co. **329.** SS; Links; Mark - Star; Thomas F. Brogan. **330.** SS; Mark - Anchor; Stern Bros. Co.

331   332   333

331. SS; Hand-punched knurling top; Unidentified. **332.** SS; Mark - 6 pt. star, 925; Portugal. **333.** SS; Mark - 6 pt. star, 925; Portugal.

334   335   336

334. SS; Mark - Mexico, 925, Iguala, Mexico, touchmark. **335.** SS; FINGERHUT MUSEUM; Mark - 8 pt. star, 925, M; Thorvald Greif. **336.** SS; Mark - P in 8 pt. star, 925; Karl-Heinz Prandl, Germany.

Catalog pages courtesy of Eleanor and Dave Brand, Metalsmiths, Dayton, Ohio.

Thimbles of Brass

Brass is essentially an alloy of copper and zinc and is one of the oldest metals used in thimble making. It is a malleable alloy which takes well to hammering, drawing, and stamping. Thimbles of brass have also been poured or molded and finished with hand or machine dressing. Brass is also suited to hand or machine chasing of designs, and can be engraved.

There are many more plain thimbles of brass to be found than those with designs. The price of a brass thimble made it accessible to most needleworkers. Brass is a strong alloy withstanding constant and hard use and was preferred by many so that competition was strong between companies selling brass thimbles. The plain brass thimble was thus a product of limiting production costs to stay ahead in the competitive market. The designed brass thimble which cost a little more may have been considered one's "Sunday Best".

The brass thimble is rarely marked with the manufacturer's name or logo. The country of origin can be found on some but most brass thimbles are unmarked.

The Thimble With The Shiny Nose

The thimble with the shiny nose
Was plain--and made of brass.
No gold or silver, I was told
Could make you sew first class.

The thimble with the shiny nose--
T'was use that made it shine.
The years of mending--sewing this and that
With stitches, Oh, so fine.

The thimble with the shiny nose
Was put on me to try,
But sewing wasn't meant for me,
I'd rather play "I Spy".

The thimble with the shiny nose
Was one my grandma wore
To stitch the blocks and make the quilts
That all came to adore.

The thimble with the shiny nose--
The Labor of Love, a symbol.
And now her sewing tool is mine--
The little plain brass thimble.

Averil Mathis

337   338   339

337. Brass; Arches; Unmarked. **338.** Brass; "Her Majesty Thimble" (Original box says "Silver Lined") England. **339.** Brass; Unmarked.

340   341   342

340. Brass; Greek Key; Unmarked. **341.** Brass; Leaf & Berry; England. **342.** Brass with threader and cutter; Unmarked.

343   344   345

343. Brass; Vintage; Unmarked. **344.** Brass; Butterfly; Unmarked. **345.** Brass; Fluted band; Unmarked.

346   347   348

346. Brass; Three tiered; Germany. **347.** Brass; Two tiered; Unmarked. **348.** Brass; Fluted; Unmarked.

349   350   351

349. Brass; Tailor's open top; Unmarked. **350.** Brass; Ring type; Mainland China. **351.** Brass; "The Prudential Life Insurance"; Unmarked.

352   353   354

352. Brass; "The Prudential Life Insurance"; Made in U.S.A. **353.** Brass; Palm leaf design; Austria. **354.** Brass; Peti-point band; Austria.

355   356   357

355. Brass; Popeye; King Features Syndicate. **356.** Brass; Olive Oyl; King Features Syndicate. **357.** Brass; Orange Bird; Walt Disney Productions.

358   359   360

358. Brass; Mickey Mouse; Walt Disney Productions. **359.** Brass; Minnie Mouse; Walt Disney Productions. **360.** Brass; Donald Duck; Walt Disney Productions.

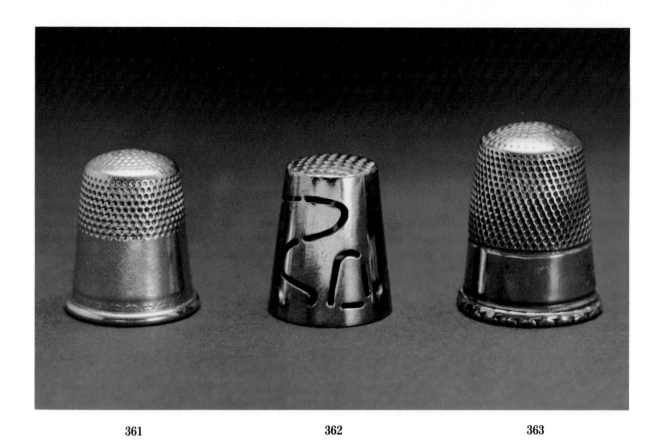

361   362   363

361. Brass; Half knurling; Unmarked. **362.** Brass; Pierced; Mark - ECB; Eleanor Brand. **363.** Brass; Floral edge; Unmarked.

364   365   366

364. Brass; Full Knurling; Unmarked. **365.** Brass; Unmarked. **366.** Brass; Fine knurling; Open top; Unmarked.

367   368   369

367. Brass; "Magic Thimble"; Pat. Dec 25, 1962; Henry Burbig. **368.** Brass; England. **369.** Brass; Germany.

370   371   372

370. Brass; Stars in Hexagons; Austria. **371.** Brass; Fan in Arches; Austria. **372.** Brass; Monopoly Game Piece (1985); Unmarked.

373   374   375

373. Brass; Leaf band; Austria. **374.** Brass; Collectors Circle Member 1982; Austria. **375.** Brass; Germany.

376   377   378

376. Brass; "Gold Thimble Scotch"; Unmarked. **377.** Brass; Iles, England (Early Iles thimble). **378.** Brass; 1982 World's Fair; Unmarked.

379   380   381

379. Brass; Child's, Unmarked. 380. Brass with cutter; Child's Unmarked. 381. Brass; Very old with top either worn out or removed; Unmarked.

382   383   384

382. Brass; Floral; Germany. 383. Brass; Basketweave; Austria. 384. Brass; Left Greek Key; Unmarked.

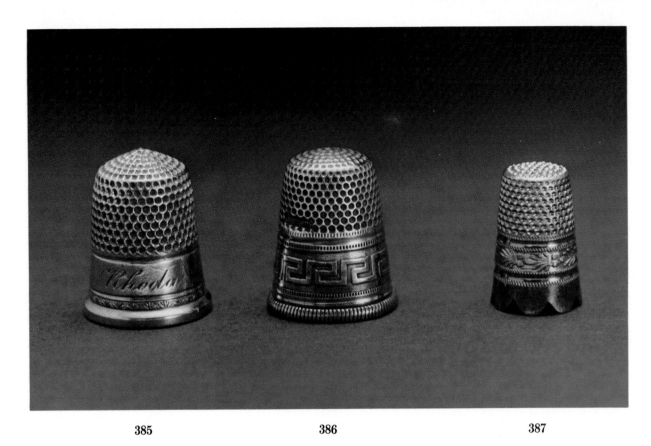

385   386   387

385. Brass; Engraved "Rhoda"; Unmarked. **386.** Brass; Right Greek Key; Germany. **387.** Brass; Child's (c. 1920).

388   389   390

388. Brass; Large knurling for heavy work; Germany. **389.** Brass; Child's; English. **390.** Brass; Feathers; England.

391   392   393

391. Brass; "Toledo"; Unmarked. **392.** Brass; Bells and Holly; Unmarked. **393.** Brass; Stars; Austria.

394   395   396

394. Brass; Child's stamped "REGARD"; Unmarked. **395.** Brass; Typical old English design; Unmarked. **396.** Brass; Applied wire with stone in center top; Nepal.

397   398   399

397. Brass with brown china cap; Holland. **398.** Brass; Mark - SDC "81"; Silver Dollar City. **399.** Brass with blue china cap; Holland.

400   401   402

400. Brass; Floral; Unmarked. **401.** Brass; Mark - 8 pt. star; Gabler, Germany. **402.** Brass; Barbed wire design; Unmarked.

403   404   405

403. Brass; Domed top; Unmarked. **404.** Brass; All over design; Unmarked. **405.** Brass with bronzed finish; Unmarked.

406   407   408

406. Brass; Basketweave; Austria. **407.** Brass; Pyramids; Unmarked. **408.** Brass; "The thimble with the shiny nose."

Thimbles of Ivory

Ivory is a product of tusks and teeth of various animals. It has been estimated that no more than 20% of the ivory used was "live ivory", or that from recently killed animals. The balance came from animals that died a natural death and is known as "dead ivory". By 1900 the stores of unearthed ivory of mammoths and mastodons had almost been depleted. It became necessary to limit ivory trade and it is now illegal in most parts of the world.

Artificial compounds were introduced as substitutes for ivory. Among these were celluloid, casein, and potatoes treated with sulfuric acid. The development in plastics has now replaced these substitutes. Careful examination will show the substitutes do not have the "grain" as does true ivory.

The first three ivory thimbles shown were brought to me from Zimbabwe, Africa in 1983, and are made from elephant tusk. Drought in Africa has reduced the forage for the elephants and many have died and other have had to be moved or destroyed. Some of this ivory has been made available to the native people who hand carve items for sale.

These thimbles are made completely with hand tools. They are first soaked in water for several days to soften the ivory. The first rough shape is made with a hand tool resembling a hoe that has been honed very sharp and used to "chop" the rough shape. Various knives and files produce the finished design and then it is polished. Note the inverted design of thimble #409.

409 410 411

412   413   414

412. Scrimshaw. 413. Scrimshaw. 414. White Camel Bone; India.

415   416

415. White Camel Bone; India. 416. Genuine Horn; Paraguay.

Thimbles of Pewter

Pewter is an alloy with a base of tin usually mixed with lead. It is very malleable and can easily be cast in molds. Occasionally brass or copper is used in the alloy in place of lead. The hardness, the look and the feel of the pewter is noticeable with the different alloy contents.

The pewter thimbles made and collected today are not functional. There are many designs in pewter thimbles ranging from classic to novelties with some made and designed by well-known artists. These pewter thimbles have a definite place in thimble collecting.

(front)   Pewter "PEEPS" thimbles   (back)

The "peep show" thimbles of the Victorian Era are being reproduced and many carry the marks shown above. The scenes depicted in three of the thimbles are shown below.

417

Woodsetton Projects, Ltd., England

418   419

420 421 422

420. Pewter; Merry-Go-Round; Nicholas Gish. **421.** Pewter; The Big Top; Nicholas Gish. **422.** Pewter on chain; Mark - C, RP; Unidentified.

423 424 425

423. Pewter; Tennessee state souvenir; Nicholas Gish. **424.** Pewter; Man-O-War (cap), Kentucky Horse Farm; Unmarked. **425.** Pewter; "Peep" Statue of Liberty; Woodsetton Projects Ltd.

426   427   428

426. Pewter; Collector Circle 1980 Member; Unmarked. **427.** Pewter; "For a Good Girl"; Unmarked. **428.** Pewter Charm; Unmarked.

429   430   431

429. Pewter; Scenic; Battersea Ltd.; England. **430.** Pewter Train; Coronodo Enterprises; Denver, CO. **431.** Pewter; Carousel; Nicholas Gish.

432   433   434

432. Pewter; Souvenir of Missouri Ozarks; Unmarked. **433.** Pewter; Egg opens, Brass bunny inside; Nicholas Gish. **434.** Pewter Stein; Souvenir 1982 World's Fair; Unmarked.

435   436   437

435. Pewter; Our Lady of Snows Shrine; Belleville, IL; Unmarked. **436.** Pewter; San Juan Capistrano; Unmarked. **437.** Pewter with China cap in blue; Holland.

90

438 439

438. Pewter; Busch Gardens; Williamsburg, VA. 439. Pewter; Edison Winter Home, Florida.

440 441

440. Pewter; Six Flags Screaming Eagle; Nicholas Gish. 441. Pewter; Gateway Arch; St. Louis, Mo; Unmarked.

Thimbles of Porcelain and China

Originally thimbles of porcelain and china were used while sewing on fine silks. The smooth surface of the glazing resisted pricking and snagging the silk. Many fine china companies made hand-painted and transfer decorated thimbles. These same procedures are still in use today.

Perhaps the most famous china thimbles are those made by MEISSEN. Some of the early ones have sold at Christie's in London for thousands of dollars. One auctioned in 1970 brought $18,000.00.

The artwork on the hand-painted thimbles is fabulous. Some of these scenes in miniature rival many of the more famous oil paintings done by the masters.

Today's porcelain and china thimbles are made mostly with the collector in mind. They do not seem to be intentionally sized, although the size will vary some. In order to purchase one for use, one must try on the thimble until the correct size is found.

Porcelain and china thimbles are being issued in series, subscribed to on a "Thimble-A-Month" club or some similar arrangement. These are today's collectors' items but may some day increase in value as many are sold as limited editions.

Catalog page courtesy of P.J.W. Thimbles, Lindau, West Germany.

442   443   444

442. China; Imari style; Touchmarked. **443.** China; Souvenir of Tennessee; Unmarked. **444.** China; Personalized; Signed and dated (Gift).

445   446   447

445. China; Roses; Unmarked. **446.** China; Blue Delft; Unmarked. **447.** China; Limoges; France.

448   449   450

448. China; Charles & Diana; Belmar; USA. **449.** China; Neuschwanstein Castle; Germany. This is the castle used as a model for Walt Disney Productions.). **450.** China; Primroses; England.

451   452   453

451. Bone China; Ashleydale; England. **452.** China; First Limited Edition; Meissen; Germany. **453.** China; Pewter Liberty Bell; Heirloom Ed.; USA.

454   455   456

454. Bone China; Hummingbird; England. **455.** Bone China; Charles & Diana; Theodore Paul, England. **456.** Jasperware; Olympiad XXIII; Wedgewood; England.

457   458   459

457. Jasperware; Josiah Wedgewood; Wedgewood; England. **458.** Bone China; Mirabelle; Wedgewood; England. **459.** China; Limited Edition; Antonio Barsato; Italy.

460 461 462

460. Bone China; Pope Paul II; Spode; England. **461.** Pottery; Lord Nelson Pottery; England. **462.** China; Ansley; England.

463 464 465

463. China; Hand painted; Betty Daley; USA. **464.** China; Christmas 1981; Caverswall; England. **465.** China; Bareuther; Germany.

466 467 468

466. China; Avon Christmas 1981; Japan. **467.** China; Royal Worcester; England. **468.** Unglazed Porcelain; Llardo'; Spain.

469 470 471

469. China; Haviland; France. **470.** China; Franciscan; USA. **471.** Bone China; Noritake; Japan.

472   473   474

472. China; Spode; England. **473.** China; Hutschenreuther; Germany. **474.** China; Ginori; Italy.

475   476   477

475. China; Mosa; The Netherlands. **476.** China; Royal Tara; Ireland. **477.** Jasperware; Wedgewood; England.

478   479   480

478. China; Bernardaud; France. 479. China; Adams; England. 480. China; Okura; Japan.

481   482   483

481. China; Staffs; England. 482. Ironstone; Johnson Brothers; England. 483. China; Coalport; England.

484   485   486

484. China; Franklin Porcelain; USA. 485. China; Masons; England. 486. China; Royal Copenhagen; Denmark.

487   488   489

487. Bone China; Royal Adderley; England. 488. China; Rorstrand; Sweden. 489. Bone China; Hammersley; England.

490   491   492

490. Bone China; Royal Albert; England. **491.** Bone China; Royal Doulton; England. **492.** Ceramic; I. Sanchez; USA.

493   494   495

493. Ironstone; Unmarked. **494.** China; Rockwell, "Day in Life of a Boy"; Japan. **495.** China; Rockwell, "Day in Life of a Boy"; Japan.

496   497   498

496. China; Rockwell, Jackrabbit; Gorham; USA. **497.** China; Rockwell, Deer; Gorham; USA. **498.** China; Rockwell, Fox; Gorham; USA.

499   500   501

499. China; Rockwell, Raccoon; Gorham; USA. **500.** China; Rockwell, Duck; Gorham; USA. **501.** China; Rockwell; Gorham; USA.

502   503   504

502. China; Hershey's Chocolate; Franklin Porcelain; USA. 503. China; Faultless Starch; Franklin Porcelain; USA. 504. China; Bon Ami Powder; Franklin Porcelain; USA.

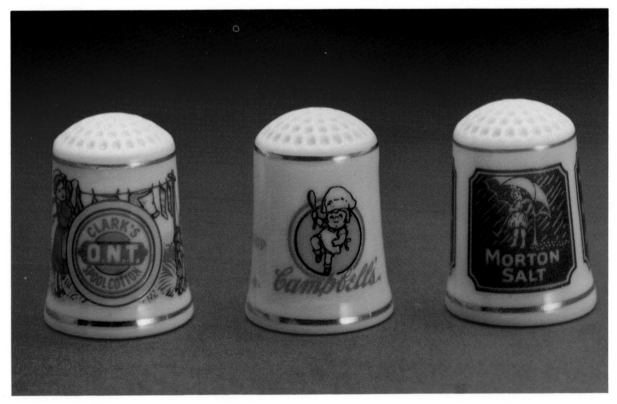

505   506   507

505. China; Clark's ONT Spool Cotton; Franklin Porcelain; USA. 506. China; Campbell's; Franklin Porcelain; USA. 507. China; Morton Salt; Franklin Porcelain; USA.

First Ladies

FIRST LADIES is a limited edition series issued by the Franklin Mint. Those ladies who served as First Ladies to the Presidents of the United States as the official Hostess are depicted. The portraits used are from the White House and from the permanent collection of the Library of Congress. They are made in fine bone china and decorated in 14K gold.

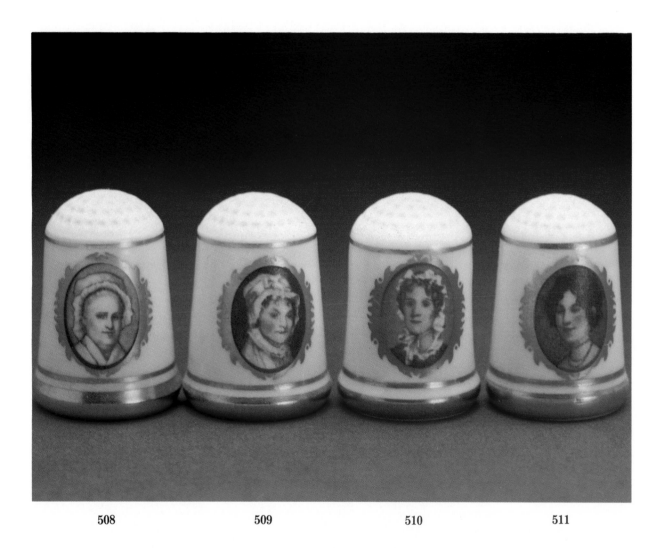

508   509   510   511

508. Martha Washington. **509.** Abigail Adams. **510.** Martha Jefferson. **511.** Dolley Madison

512   513   514   515

512. Elizabeth Monroe. 513. Louisa Adams. 514. Sarah Jackson. 515. Emily Donelson (Both Sarah Jackson and Emily Donelson served during Andrew Jackson's term)

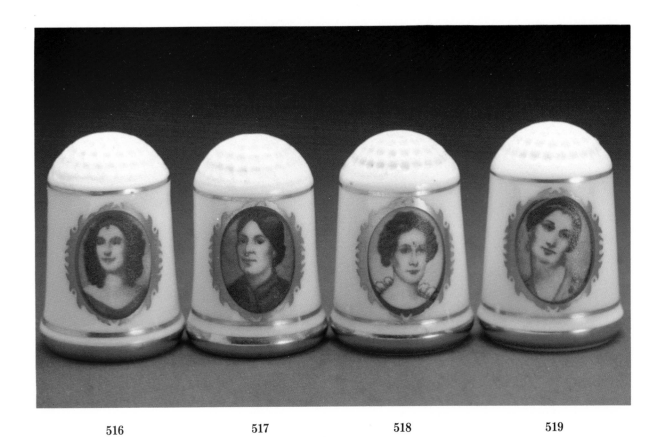

516   517   518   519

516. Angelica Van Buren (Daughter-In-Law). 517. Anna Harrison. 518. Letitia Tyler (1st wife). 519. Julia Tyler (2nd wife)

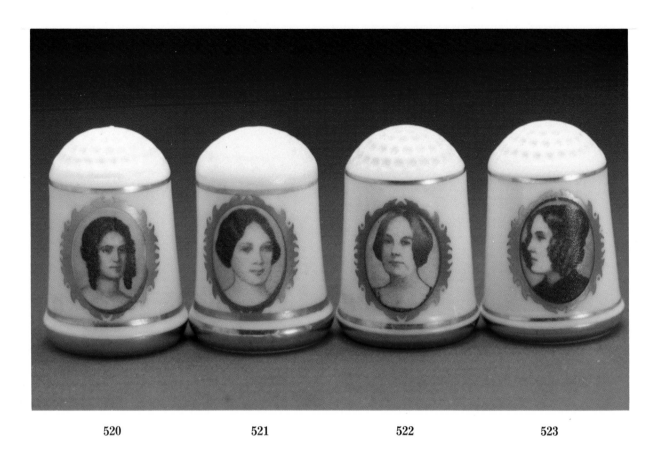

520　　　　　　521　　　　　　522　　　　　　523

520. Sarah Polk. 521. Elizabeth ''Betty'' Bliss (daughter of Zachary Taylor). 522. Abigail Fillmore; 523. Jane Pierce

524　　　　　　525　　　　　　526　　　　　　527

524. Mary Todd Lincoln. 525. Harriet Lane (Niece of James Buchanan). 526. Eliza Johnson. 527. Julia Grant

528   529   530   531

528. Lucy Hayes; 529. Lucretia Garfield. 530. Mary Arthur McElroy (Sister of Chester Arthur). 531. Frances Cleveland

532   533   534   535

532. Caroline Harrison. 533. Mary Harrison McKee; (Caroline (wife) and Mary (daughter) both served under B. Harrison. 534. Ida McKinley. 535. Edith Roosevelt

536   537   538   539

536. Helen Taft. **537.** Ellen Wilson (1st wife of Woodrow Wilson). **538.** Edith Wilson (2nd wife of Woodrow Wilson). **539.** Florence Harding

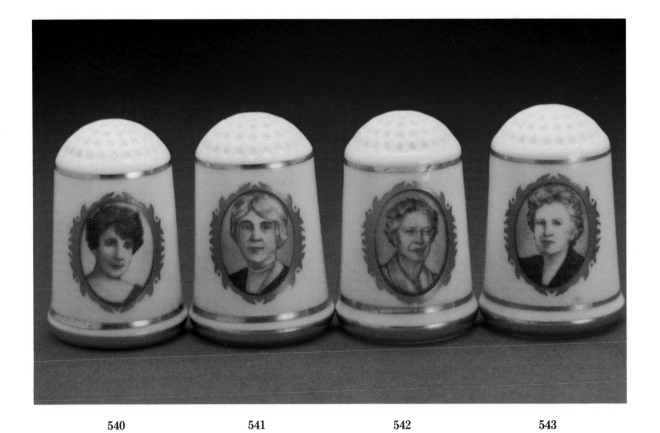

540   541   542   543

540. Grace Coolidge. **541.** Lou Hoover. **542.** Anna Eleanor Roosevelt. **543.** Bess Truman

544   545   546   547

544. Mamie Eisenhower. **545.** Jacqueline Kennedy. **546.** "Lady Bird" Johnson. **547.** "Pat" Nixon

548   549   550

548. Elizabeth "Betty" Ford. **549.** Rosalynn Carter. **550.** Nancy Reagan

The Museum of American Folk Art presents

THE AMERICAN HEIRLOOM QUILT THIMBLES

*A collection of twenty-five fine porcelain thimbles —
each portraying one of our most famous traditional quilt designs
—and each embellished with pure 24 karat gold.*

Advertising leaflet courtesy of Franklin Mint, Franklin Center, Pa.

Advertising Thimbles

Advertising thimbles are an entity withing themselves. These thimbles normally carry lettering and sometimes a logo. They are made primarily of plastic or aluminum, then comes brass and occasionally base metal. There have been some silver advertising thimbles made but these are difficult to find, therefore they carry a premium value.

Advertising thimbles are used as give-aways for good will. There are not as quickly thrown away as a pamphlet or business card as evidenced by the number that are being collected. There are some collectors who specialize in collecting advertising thimbles.

This type advertising was used by all kinds of businesses. Politicans have used them in campaigns and there are religious thimbles with Bible verses. Many collectors have their own personalized thimbles which they trade with other collectors.

Some of these thimbles are amusing. There is one that advertises FURNITURE AND UNDERTAKING. Somehow these don't seem to go together. You can turn up all kinds of surprises in advertising thimbles.

Collecting and cataloging advertising thimbles seems to be easier than thimbles with designs. The wording of the advertisement, color and composition of the thimble are the main focus points. Cataloging advertisers by alphabetical order with a notation of color is the general preference. Divisions of plastic and of the aluminum or other compositions may be made. With a small notebook this "file" can easily be carried in the purse for instant reference and can eliminate duplicate purchases.

The whistle thimble is a novelty shaped like a long thimble with a spinner whistle built into one end. It is collected as a thimble. These novelties were made of aluminum with a colored band at the bottom carrying an advertisement, and used as give-aways. They were also used for promotion in many political campaigns.

The first whistle pictured advertising NATIONAL WHITE ROSE GASOLINE is marked B&B PAT 2092942.

551.   552.

553.   554.

551. National White Rose Gasoline.

552. Drink Orange Crush for Health.

553. Groves Shoe Company

554. Wagner Beer

555 556 557

555. Red top Plastic; Political; Elect Henry L. Mueller. **556.** Plastic; Political; Vote Straight Republican. **557.** Plastic; Political; Jimmy Carter for President.

558 559 560

558. Plastic; Religious; Bible verse. **559.** Plastic; Advertising; The Lamp Works. **560.** Plastic; Advertising; Sew and Save The Singer Way.

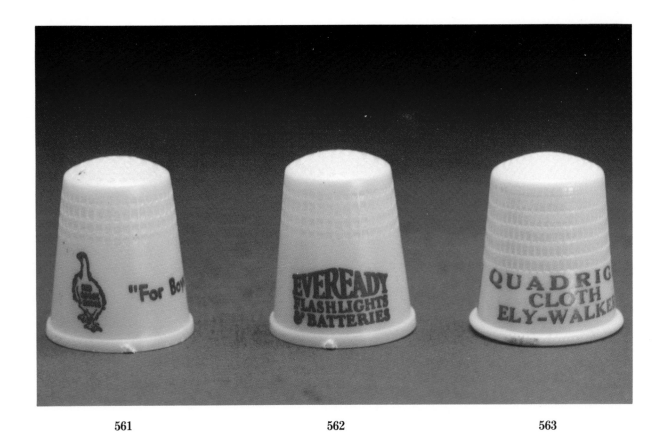

561   562   563

561. Plastic; Advertising; Red Goose Shoes. **562.** Plastic; Advertising; Eveready Flashlights & Batteries. **563.** Plastic; Advertising; Quadrigua Cloth; Ely-Walker.

564   565   566

564. Plastic; Political; Elect Reagan President 1980. **565.** Plastic; Advertising; John Deere. **566.** Plastic; Woodmen of the World.

567   568   569

567. Plastic; Advertising; Sinclair Oils. **568.** Plastic; Advertising; Lady Madison Shops. **569.** Plastic; Advertising; Hadacol.

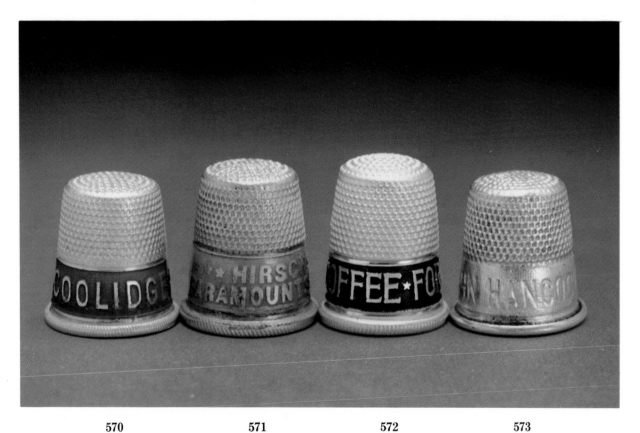

570   571   572   573

570. Aluminum; Political; Coolidge & Dawes. **571.** Aluminum; Advertising; Hirsch's Goodies. **572.** Aluminum; Advertising; Forbes Coffee. **573.** Aluminum; Advertising; Hancock Mutual Life.

574   575   576   577

574. Aluminum; Advertising; White Sewing Machines. 575. Aluminum; Advertising; Iten's Bisquit Co.
576. Aluminum; Advertising; Wear Topsy Hosiery. 577. Aluminum; Advertising; Enna Jettick Shoes.

578   579   580   581

578. Aluminum; Hoover-Home-Happiness. 579. Aluminum; Advertising; Clements Electric Vacuum Cleaners.
580. Aluminum; Advertising; Prairie Queen Flour. 581. Aluminum; Advertising; White King Soap.

582   583   584   585

582. Aluminum; Advertising; Star Brand Shoes. 583. Aluminum; Advertising; Red Goose Shoes. 584. Aluminum; Advertising; Geo. C. Lang, Furniture & Undertaking. 585. Aluminum; Advertising; 1892 Ware that Wears.

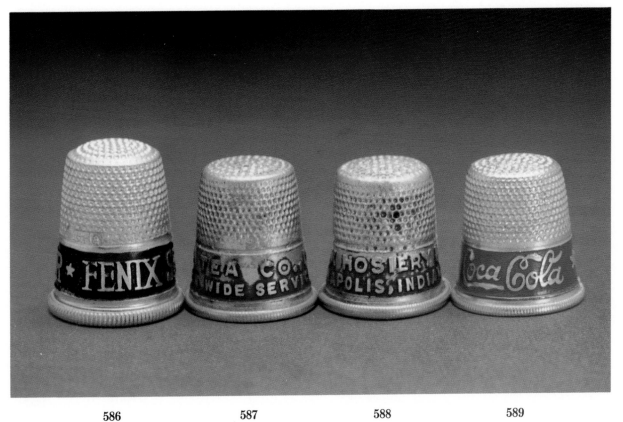

586   587   588   589

586. Aluminum; Advertising; Fenix Self Rising Flour. 587. Aluminum; Advertising; Jewel Tea Co. 588. Aluminum; Advertising; Real Silk Hosiery Mills 589. Aluminum; Advertising; Drink Coca-Cola.

590 591 592

590. Aluminum; Advertising; Singer Sewing Machines. 591. Base Metal; Advertising; IDEAL. 592. Plated Brass; Advertising; Prudential Life Insurance.

593 594 595

593. Sterling Silver; Advertising; Domestic Sewing Machines. 594. Sterling Silver; TORREMOLINOS. 595. Sterling Silver; Marked JW Ltd., Wheat Sheaves, Lion, B, ZI; "James Walker, The London Jeweller."

Collectibles and Novelties

Many different alloys were used to make thimbles for everyday use. Some were nickel-silver, nickel plated brass, steel, iron, aluminum and brass. The brass thimbles are dealt with separately.

Alloy thimbles are the mainstay of the needleworkers. They may have little or no decoration in order to minimize the cost of production and be sold in a competitive market. Only a few of these metal thimbles are marked. Some have only the country of origin stamped on them and others have no mark other than the size.

Simons Bros. Co. of Philadelphia marked their industrial thimbles made from 1919 to 1952. This mark was different from the mark they used on their gold and silver thimbles. The industrial thimble was marked in the apex by a keystone and SBC within a thimble and with USA above, as shown in the marks section.

Thimbles of Poland are found stamped with the selling price. In this state-run economy the government dictates the selling price and it is stamped directly on the thimble. The coinage is *Zloty* and the mark on the thimble is ZL 2.80 found on the band. The size is stamped on the top of the thimble.

A lining was used in some thimbles. This double wall thimble process was used mainly on the older steel and iron thimbles since these metals were hard on the fingers. To eliminate this factor, thimbles were lined with brass or aluminum and the strength of the thimble remained.

Aluminum thimbles are normally too soft to be used as an everday working thimble. Many of the aluminum thimbles found have been part of a sewing or mending kit and so used for emergency sewing only. Aluminum was also used extensively in the production of advertising thimbles. The low price, however, did sell many aluminum thimbles.

There are thimbles of wood, glass, papier mache', plastic and many other materials made to appeal to the thimble collector. Many of these are simply novelties which have the appearance of a thimble but are not truly functional. There seems to be a large demand for this type thimble and new ones are constantly entering the market.

596 597 598

596. Base Metal; Advertising. **597.** Copper; Pear-shaped knurling. **598.** Base Metal; Germany.

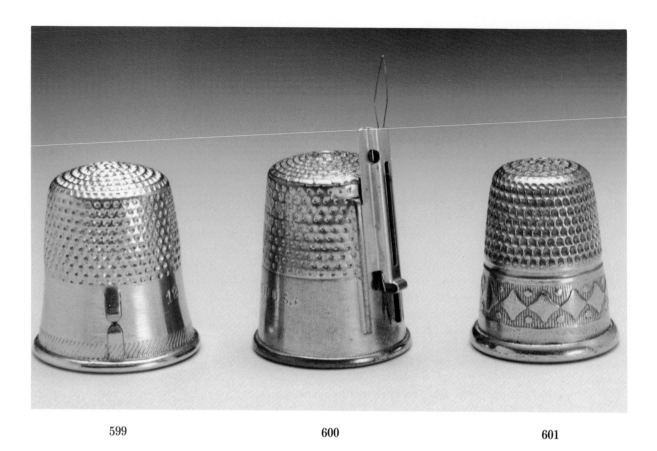

599   600   601

599. Base Metal; Thread cutter. 600. Base Metal; Cutter and Threader; Marked: MT PAT'D, Made in USA. 601. Metal; England.

602   603   604

602. Metal; Star on cap. 603. Metal; Star on cap. 604. Metal; Star on cap.

605   606   607

605. Metal; Star on cap. **606.** Alloy; Marked with Simons SBC logo. **607.** Alloy; Marked with Simons SBC logo.

608   609   610

608. Alloy; Marked with Simons SBC logo. **609.** Metal; Tailor's with fine knurling; Unmarked. **610.** Steel with aluminum lining; Tailor's; Unmarked.

611   612   613

611. Steel; Brass lined, Tailor's; Germany. 612. Steel; (very old) Tailor's; Unmarked. 613. Abalone/Brass; Mexico.

614   615   616

614. Abalone/Brass; Mexico. 615. Abalone/Brass; Mexico. 616. Metal; Child's thimble.

617   618   619   620

617. Wooden; Personalized; Made by Author. **618.** Wooden; Hand painted; USA. **619.** Aspen Wood; Rolled paper message inside. **620.** Crocheted; Made by Author.

621   622   623

621. Metal; England. **622.** Metal; England. **623.** Metal; Unmarked.

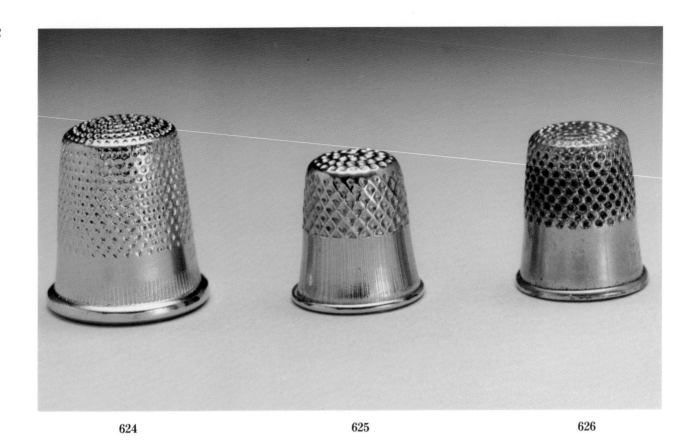

624   625   626

624. Metal; Spain. **625.** Metal; Child's size 3; Poland. **626.** Metal; Marked ZL 2.80; Poland.

627   628   629

627. Metal; Diamond knurling; Poland. **628.** Metal; Diamond knurling; Poland. **629.** Metal; Diamond knurling; Poland.

630 631 632

630. Metal; Tailor's with large knurling; Unmarked. **631.** Steel (very thin); Tailor's; Round knurling; Unmarked. **632.** Leather Quilter's thimble; USA.

633 634 635

633. Steel/Brass lined; Unmarked. **634.** Pewter (Gilded); "For a Good Girl"; Unmarked. **635.** Metal; "Dorothy" thimble; Iles; England.

636   637   638

636. Charms (Belonged to author's twin daughters); Marked: STG, JMF. **637.** Metal; "Dorothy" thimble; Iles; England. **638.** Metal/Cutter; Marked: Pat. Pend; ST (on cap); Unidentified.

639   640   641

639. Cloisonné; Unmarked. **640.** Cloisonné; Unmarked. **641.** Bronze; Membership Collector Circle 1981; Fort; USA.

642   643   644

642. Metal; Germany. **643.** Aluminum/Brass lined. **644.** Aluminum/Brass lined.

645   646   647

645. Steel; (Heavy) Tailor's; England. **646.** Aluminum; Unmarked. **647.** Copper/"Majestic" Aladdin Lamp (applied); Custom made by author.

648   649   650   651

648. Teak Wood; Thimble and holder; India. 649. Oak wood; Hand painted, signed, dated; USA. 650. Olive wood; Jerusalem (gift). 651. Wood; Painted; Anri.

652   653   654

652. Leaded glass; West Germany. 653. Glass; Coca-Cola. 654. Glass; Mary Gregory type; Italy.

655   656   657

655. Glass; Etched bells; USA. **656.** Glass; Etched grapes with scalloped edge; USA. **657.** Glass; Painted; Unmarked.

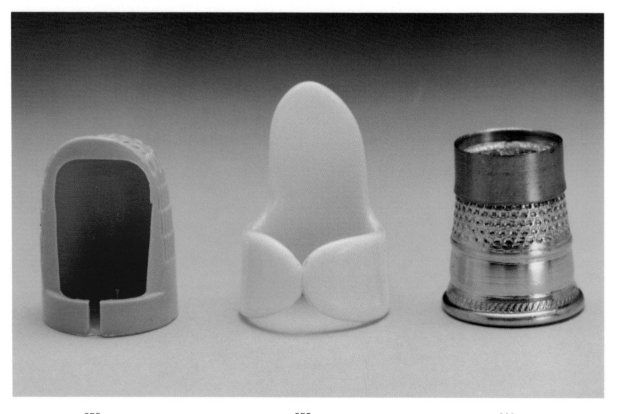

658   659   660

658. Plastic; Adjustable; Pat. No. 208047; USA. **659.** Plastic; Quilter's Finger Guard. **660.** Metal/Brass band at top (quilter's needle guard); USA.

661   662   663

661. Metal/Cutter; Threader; Star on cap; Unmarked. **662.** Metal; Early Iles design. **663.** Gilded Aluminum; Two tier; Unmarked.

664   665   666

664. Alloy; Simons SBC logo; Simons Bros. Co. **665.** Gilded plastic/Magnet top. **666.** Brass; Bluebells on dark ground; Unmarked.

667   668   669

667. Alloy; Simons SBC logo; Simons Bros. Co. **668. and 669.** Enamel on Brass; Mother-Daughter set; Austria.

670   671   672

670. Metal/Cutter; Unmarked. **671.** Metal/Mother & Child shield; USA. **672.** Fashioned from Coal; USA.

673   674   675

673. Aluminum/Stone top; Austria. **674.** Aluminum; Unmarked. **675.** Aluminum; Unmarked.

676   677   678

676 through 681. Aluminum, various sizes and designs. Sold as a group known as a "Quilter's nest".

679   680   681

676 through 681. Aluminum, various sizes and designs. Sold as a group know as a "Quilter's nest".

682   683

682. Aluminum; Unmarked. **683.** Aluminum; Unmarked.

684   685   686

684. Glass; Unmarked. **685.** Glass; Unmarked. **686.** Millefiori Glass; Italy.

687   688   689

687. Alabaster; Unmarked. **688.** Murano Glass; Italy. **689.** Glass; Unmarked.

690　　　　　　　　　691　　　　　　　　　692

690. Quilter's Leather Guard; USA. 691. Clerk's Rubber finger stall; England. 692. Quilter's Leather Guard; USA.

693. Sailor's Palm

Thimble Cases and Holders

Thimble cases and thimble holders are made from a variety of materials. When a thimble was given as a gift, many times it had its own case, holder or box. The case may have had a ring attached to be hung on a chain as a necklace or from a chatelain. Some were made to be carried in pocket or purse as a thimble protector. Many of these cases had matching thimbles though few of these matched sets have survived. Special presentation boxes were made lined with satin or plush, and some with a post to hold the thimble in place. Original presentation boxes are unique collector's items.

There are holders made of brass, china, glass and other materials. Some may be characterized as whimsical or novelty, but they are all a part of the overall picture of thimble collecting.

694. 800 Silver, Bee's wax and thimble holder, Germany.

695   696

695. SS; Thread Case; Mark - Lion, Anchor, Letter date; England. **696.** Walnut wood thimble case; Unmarked.

697   698

697. and 698. Embossed metal thimble cases (c. 1890); England.

699   700

699. Leather, plush-lined thimble case; Unmarked. **700.** Wicker basket; Unmarked.

701   702

701. Sterling/Gold; Acorn thimble holder; Tiffany. **702.** Sterling; Egg thimble holder; Thought to be Russian.

703   704

703. SS, Gold interior; Unger Bros; USA. **704.** Sterling; Unmarked.

705   706

705. SS; Thimble holder; Mark - Lion facing right, Anchor; England. **706.** SS/Plush lined thimble holder; Tiffany.

707   708

707. Sterling, Gold-plated Strawberry thimble holder; Tiffany. 708. Sterling Thimble Holder; Unger Bros.

709   710

709. Original Presentation box with Thimble #263. 710. SS/Gold plated interior; Octagon Thimble holder, Foster & Bailey.

711   712

711. Brass, Applied wire, Blood Ruby stone; Thimble holder; India. 712. Cloisonné Thimble Holder; China.

713   714

713. Mother of Pearl/Brass Thimble holder; Unmarked. 714. Sterling Pierced design Thimble Holder; Webster Co.

715   716

715. Sterling, Pierced, Plain top for engraving; Holder; Webster Co. **716.** Sterling Thimble Holder; Gorham.

717   718

717. Silver Plated Thimble Holder; Silvermans. **718.** Sweet grass Thimble Holder.

719   720

719. Sterling Holder, Original thimble engraved 1870. **720.** Vegetable Ivory Thimble and **case**; Unmarked.

721. Vegetable Ivory Thimble and case.

722. Vegetable Ivory Thimble and Case; Unmarked.

723. Shell holder, Thimble by Simons Bros. Co.; Sold as souvenir at World's Columbian Exposition, Chicago, Illinois, 1893.

724   725

724. Casket type, red Leatherette presentation case; Thimble #287. **725.** Casket type brown leatherette case; Thimble #33.

726   727

726. Plush lined presentation case; Thimble #29. **727.** Round, satin lined presentation case; Thimble #41.

728. Top

728. Thimble holder made for Silver Cased Thimble made by Iles of England. Bottom shows the three thimble trademark.

Bottom

729. China holder with matching thimble; Reuter; Germany.

730. China; Thimble holder with matching thimble inside; Unmarked.

731. Matching Thimble and Needle case; Mount Royal China; England.

Mending Kits

Mending kits are made of everything from precious metal to plastic. They come in designer items and are also made for advertising give-aways. The kit design may change with need or cultural and fad changes, but the components remain fairly stable. Because they contain thimbles, they become very much a part of thimble collecting.

732. World War I Sewing Kit.

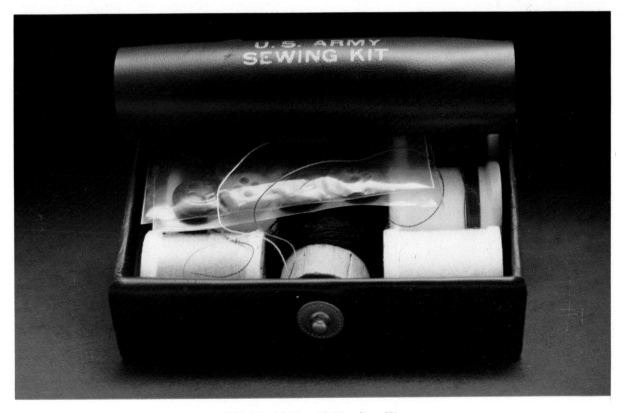

733. World War II Mending Kit.

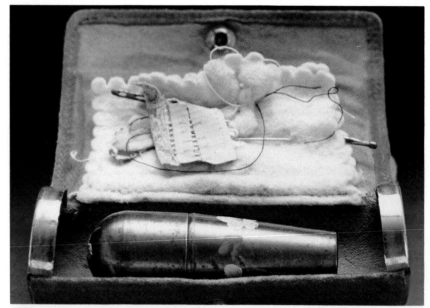

734. Suede Roll-over kit with bullet-type holder.

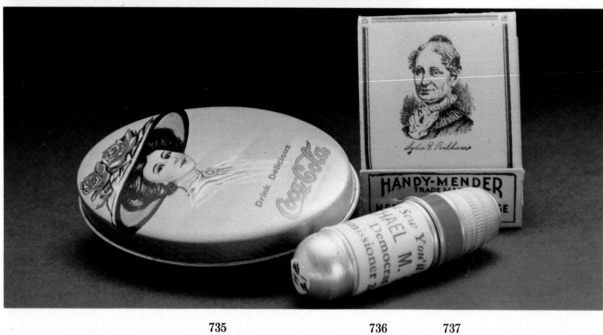

735   736   737

735. Coca-Cola mending kit; Unmarked. **736.** Political; Michael Sweeney. **737.** Lydia Pinkham needle and thread case.

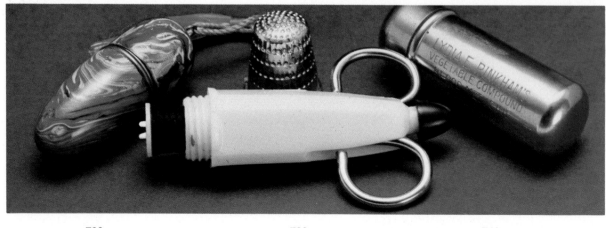

738   739   740

738. Enameled Brass mending kit; Germany. **739** Plastic mending kit; Unmarked. **740.** Lydia Pinkham's mending kit.

741   743   742

741. Brass; Beier's Bread; Mending kit; Germany. **742.** Firestone (Advertising not shown); celluloid. **743.** Purple celluloid mending kit; Germany.

744   745

744. Plastic Doll mending kit; Unmarked. **745.** Mending kit resembling lighter; Germany.

746   747   748

746. Plated brass mending kit; Austria. **747.** Embossed metal mending kit with brass thimble; Germany. **748.** Gilded brass, Needlepoint top mending kit; Austria.

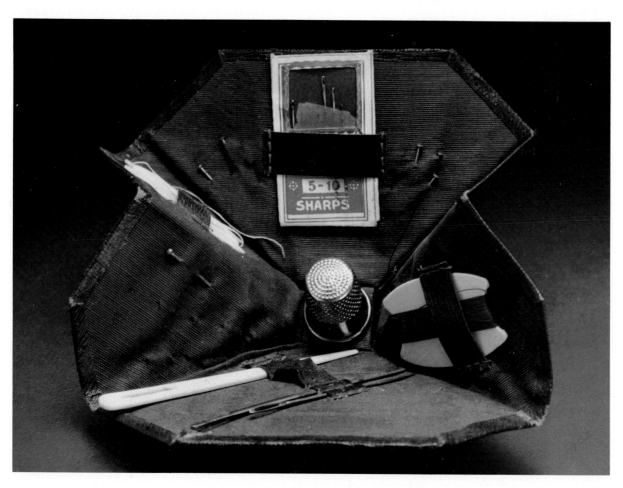

749. Folding mending kit with ivory fittings.

Sewing Accessories

Some collectors enjoy adding other sewing items to their collection. Elaborately fitted cases for sewing that were once so popular contained many of these sewing items. Some of these cases contained matching ivory items while others were fitted with precious metal components. There are very few of these cases found with all the pieces intact and it becomes necessary to collect them as individual pieces.

Smaller matched sets are more easily found. These sets primarily consisted of thimble, scissor and needle case.

Other accessories were made to assist the needle-worker. Some of these items have been included.

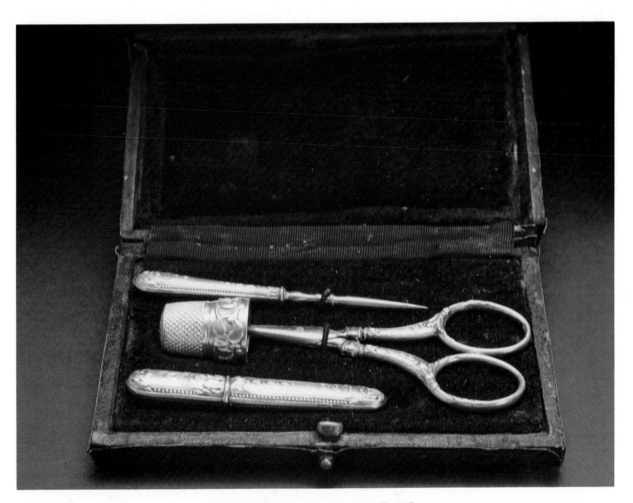

750. SS; Matched Sewing set; French.

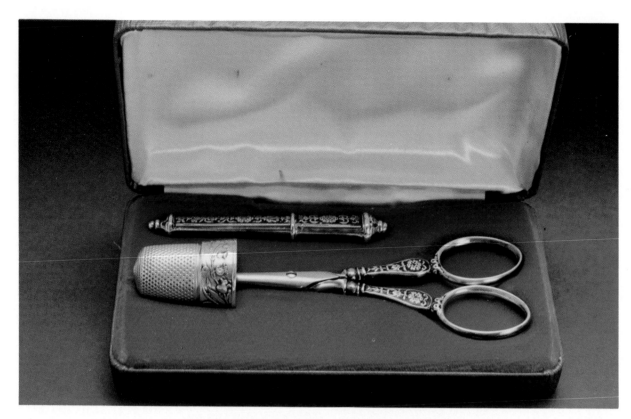

751. SS; Matched Sewing set; P. Lenain; France.

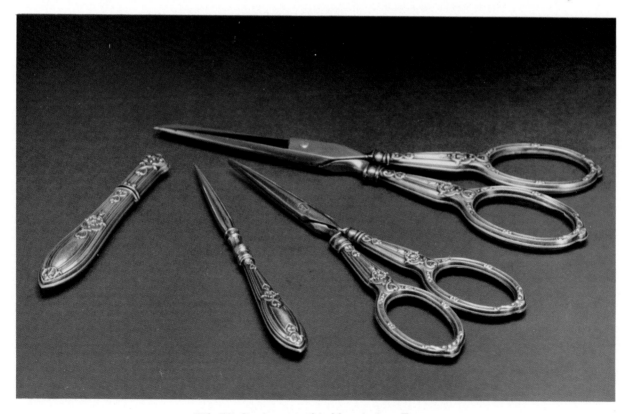

752. SS; Sewing set; thimble missing; France.

753   754

753. SS; Pin cushion; Mark - D&LS, Lion, Anchor, n; English. **754.** Silver plated thread holder; Wilcox.

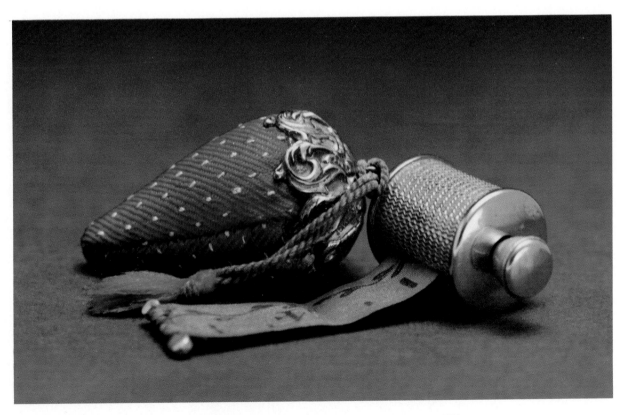

755   756

755. Sterling top strawberry emery; Unmarked. **756.** Sterling tape measure; Unmarked.

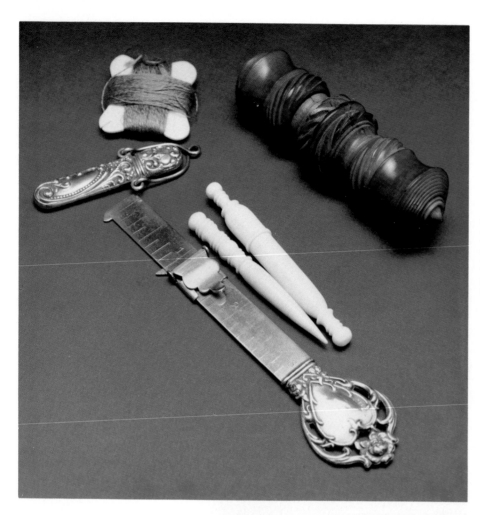

Clockwise: 757. Vegetable Ivory Needle Case. **758.** Ivory Needle case. **759.** Ivory Stiletto. **760.** SS Measuring gauge. **761.** SS Needle case (from Chatelain). **762.** Ivory Thread Winder.

Left to right:
763. SS Tatting Shuttle; Nussbaum & Hunold. **764.** Sterling handled egg darner. **765.** Sterling adjustable stiletto.

766. "Nellie" Thimble Servant

767. "Louise All-In-One"

768. Wooden sewing box; Two drawers, pincushion unit lifts to insert spools of thread dispensed through eyelets.

769. Plush sewing box; satin interior, ivory fittings.

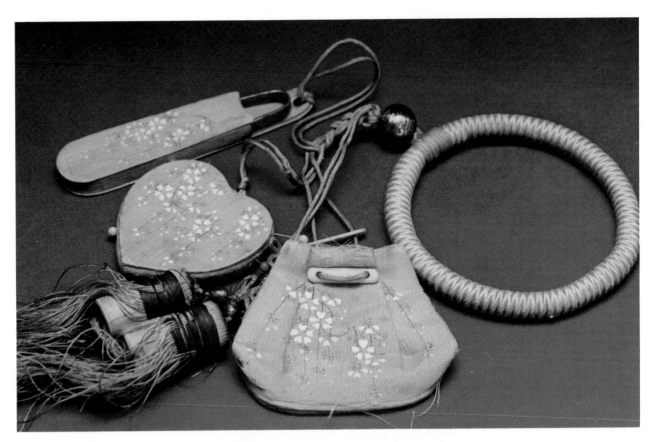

770. Silk Chatalaine; Ring loops over sash.

771. Clark's ONT Spool Cotton sewing box; Marked and dated; Charles Tollner, 1890, Hackensack, N.J.

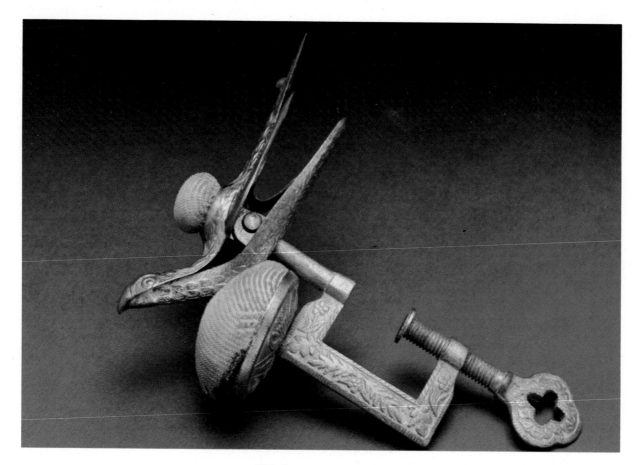

772. Brass Sewing Bird.

773 774

773. Ivory clamp pin cushion. 774. Cast Iron Quilter's clamp (four were used).

775   776

775. Sterling Glove Darner; Webster. **776.** Sterling Glove Darner; Unmarked.

777. Brass Needle Holder; Unmarked.

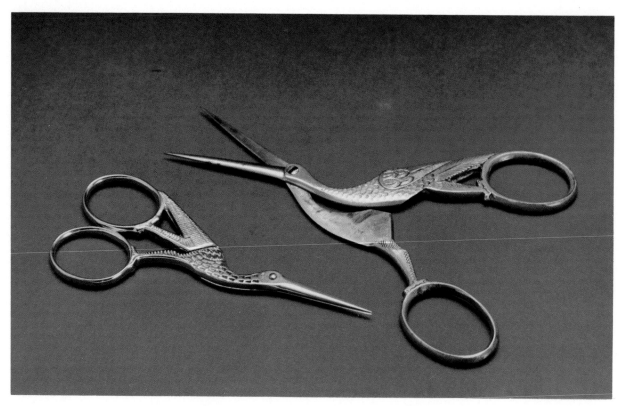

778   779

778. Stork Scissor; Brass; Italy. **779.** Stork Scissor; Steel; Germany.

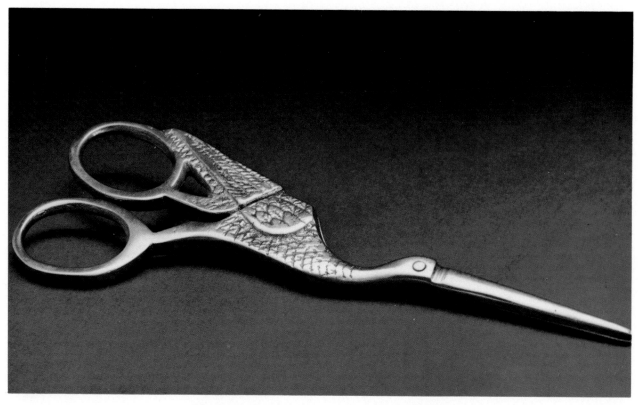

780. Stork Scissor; Brass, 7″ overall; Unmarked.

781. Goat cart thimble holder; Unmarked.

782   783

782. Hallmark Christmas Angel; Fourth in series. 783. Hallmark Christmas Angel; Seventh in series.

784. Glass shoe thimble holder.

785. China shoe thimble holder.

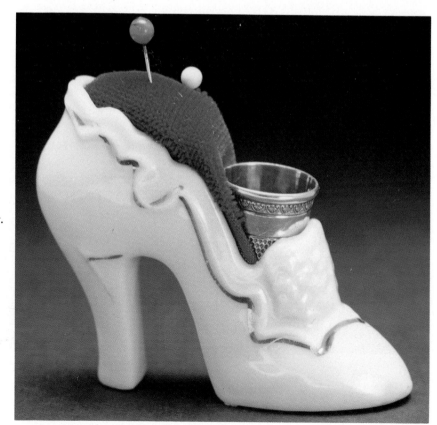

786   787

786. China thimble minder; Unmarked. **787.** Pewter thimble stand.

788   789

788. Pewter figural thimble stand; Unmarked. **789.** Rooster; Bronze thimble stand; Austria.

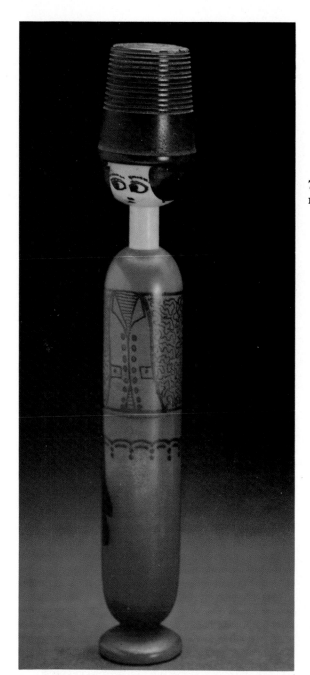

790. Wooden doll; thimble holder & needle case; Unmarked.

791. Cast Iron; Gilded Thread Holder.

792 793

792. Stickware Mending Egg. **793.** Darner with metal strap.

794. Mini Hen on nest thimble holder.

795. Sterling Silver Jigger; Charles Thomae & Sons.

Marks

There are two sections of marks. The first deals with metals and is listed by countries of origin. The second section deals with china and pottery.

Some variations will be noted in the marks on the thimbles. The company mark was sometimes simplified for use on thimbles or the striking may be imperfect. The angle of light used to view the mark may change the looks. The size of the mark and the wear may also alter the appearance. Some companies are known to have made minor changes in their marks through the years of manufacture.

Section One - Metals

American thimbles are generally marked by the company's trademark, many of which are registered. In an effort to copy English Hallmarks, some companies used a series of marks which are called pseudo-hallmarks. The standard silver content of .925 fine silver is marked STERLING.

England has an extensive Hallmark system with assay offices in major cities. Random pieces were sent for assay before polishing. The Hallmarks include the (1) sponsor's (maker) mark of first and last initial, (2) assay office, (3) Lion passant (mark for .925 fine silver), and (4) date letter. Charts are needed for dating.

French thimbles carry a Mercury head for .925 fine silver. Thimbles made in Paris are marked with a Boar's head and a crab for the provinces. Silversmiths use a touchmark to identify their work.

Swedish thimbles are marked with a trefoil containing three crowns. An S in a hexagon denotes .925 fine silver. City marks and date marks are used and charts are needed for identification. Initials identify the silversmith.

Silversmiths in Italy are registered with the government and this registration number is stamped on the thimble. Some thimbles carry the makers intials also. The fineness content is stamped on the thimble.

A four or a five pointed star usually represents Portugal. The cockerel and silver fineness are found on some of the thimbles from Portugal.

German thimbles are found to carry a six pointed and an eight pointed star. The silver content may be stamped on the thimble along with other markings.

Some entries will carry a location where the mark might be found. This location will vary at times so it is advisable to look inside the apex, on the band, inside the lip, in the first rows of knurling and on the top or cap of the thimble for marks.

AMERICA

A.L.&Co.

(band)
Aiken, Lambert & Co.
New York, N.Y.

BN Co.

(in apex)
Baird-North Co. (Jobbers)
Providence, R.I.

(band)
Barker Mfg. Co.
Providence, R.I.

(band)
E. & J. Bass
New York, N.Y.

David Brand

ECB

Eleanor Brand

(inside)
Dayton, Ohio

(band or in apex)
Thomas F. Brogan
New York, N.Y.

(in apex)
Carter, Sloan & Co.
Carter, Howe & Co.
Carter, Gough & Co.
New York, N.Y.

Foster & Bailey
Providence, R.I.

(band or in apex)
Goldsmith, Stern & Co.
New York, N.Y.

Gorham Corp.
Providence, R.I.

(in apex)
Ketcham & McDougall
New York, N.Y.

o· 10K Gold

MERMOD JACCARD CO. PURE COIN

(band)
Mermod, Jaccard Co.
St. Louis, MO

Sterling and Gold

Mark for Gold Filled

(band)
H. Muhr's Sons
Philadelphia, PA

Joseph Muhr

Nussbaum & Hunold
Providence, R.I.

N. & H.

S

(band)
Shepard Mfg. Co.
Melrose Highlands, Mass.

(in apex)
D.C. Percival & Co.
Boston, Mass.
(Made by Waite-Thresher)

Simons Bros. Co.
Philadelphia, Pa.

(in apex)
Simons Industrial
18% Nickel
60% Copper
22% Zinc
Made 1919 to 1952

(in apex)
Trefoil, used on gold plate

(in apex)
Mark for 14K Gold

(in apex)
Priscilla

(in apex)
Silver Filled

Mark for Gold Filled

Stern Bros. Co.
New York, N.Y.

Charles Thomae & Sons
Attleboro, Mass.

TIFFANY & C⚥

Tiffany & Co., Inc.
New York, N.Y.

Towle Silversmiths
Newburyport, Mass.

Unger Bros.
Newark, N.Y.

(in apex)
Waite-Thresher
Providence, R.I.

(band or in apex)
Webster Co.
N. Attleboro, Mass.

English Sponsor's Marks

James Fenton

Wilcox Silverplate Co.
Meriden, Conn.

H G & S

H G & S DREEMA

Henry Griffith & Sons

ENGLAND

(marks generally on band)

Assay Offices

London

Edinburgh

Birmingham

Sheffield

Chester

CH **8**
DORCAS

Dorcas

CH Silver

PAT. 10 Early Dorcas

Charles Horner

Charles Iles, Sr.
Birmingham, England

Sterling Marks

English Sterling Mark

1935 Silver Jubilee Mark

1953 Coronation Mark

1977 Silver Jubilee Mark

S J R & S

S.J. Rose & Sons

J S & S

J. Swan & Son

James Walker, Ltd.

Woodsetton Projects Ltd.
West Midlands, England

GERMANY

National Reich Silvermark (old)

Gabler (on cap)

(on cap) (in Knurling)
Helmut & Thorvald Greif

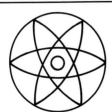

Lotthammer-Eber (on cap)

J.A. Henckels (in knurling)
Made by Lotthammer-Eber

Karl-Heinz Prandl (on cap)

FRANCE

Mercury Head (.925 fine silver)

P. Lenain

THE NETHERLANDS

Import mark for .925 silver **ZI**

SWEDEN

Made in Sweden   City Mark of Falun   Date mark 1947

Silver mark (.925 fine)   Maker's mark (unidentified)

ITALY
(Examples from thimbles-unidentified)

MEXICO
(Examples from thimbles-unidentified)

MEXICO SILVER

PORTUGAL
(Examples from thimbles-unidentified)

Unidentified Marks

Thimble Nos. 15,27,47

JUDD   Thimble No. 113

H&S   Thimble No. 129

(on Ketcham & McDougall Thimble)

LAMSON   Thimble No. 254

S. BROS.   Thimble No. 290

Thimble No. 291   H.W. LTD

Thimble No. 638   JMF STG

Item No. 724

Item No. 776   D&LS

Adams, England

Aynsley, England

Bareuther, Germany

Belmar, USA

B & C°   Bernardaud, France

©BETTY DALEY   Betty Daley, USA

Coalport, England

Franciscan, USA

Franklin Porcelain, USA

FRANKLIN PORCELAIN

Ginori, Italy

Gorham, USA

Hammersley, England

Hutschenreuther, Germany

Johnson Bros., England

Llardo, Spain

Lord Nelson Pottery, England

Masons, England

Meissen, Germany

Mosa, The Netherlands

Noritake, Japan

Okura, Japan

Reuter, Germany

Rorstrand, Sweden

Royal Adderley, England

Royal Albert, England

Royal Copenhagen, Denmark

Royal Doulton, England

Royal Tara, Ireland

Royal Worcester, England

Spode, England

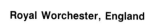

WEDGWOOD

Staffs (Wedgwood group), England

Wedgwood, England

Photo

No._____

Desc. _____

_____Size _____

Engraving _____

Mfg. _____

Country _____

Marks

Reference _____

Bought _____

Cost_____Date _____

Photo

No._____

Desc. _____

_____Size _____

Engraving _____

Mfg. _____

Country _____

Marks

Reference _____

Bought _____

Cost_____Date _____

Photo

No._____

Desc. _____

_____Size _____

Engraving _____

Mfg. _____

Country _____

Marks

Reference _____

Bought _____

Cost_____Date _____

Design

by
Averil Mathis

for

A.Q.S. THIMBLE

FIG. 1

FIG. 2

Thimble designed by Averil Mathis for
The American Quilter's Society.
Production scheduled to begin in 1986.

Value Guide

You may wish to use the values listed as a guide to approximate the worth of a thimble. Prices will vary in different parts of the country, and with many of the dealers. The amount of precious metal in a thimble is negligible so the real value is in the design, the maker, the condition and the rarity.

The figure following the description indicates an average dollar price of a thimble with no dents or holes and with only average wear with the design clearly visible. A thimble with holes, dents, cracks or worn design-- any one or a combination of these factors would lessen the value. A better than average thimble that shows very little wear would be of greater value, while one in "mint" condition would carry a premium value. There are some thimbles of choice design or rare maker's marks that are hard to find. These would command an even greater premium value.

To obtain a value trend in your area, visit antiques shows and flea markets and examine the thimbles. Note the design, condition and maker along with the price. You may wish to consult trade papers for a broader value trend.

When buying a thimble, know your marks and be sure the thimble is what is advertised. Most dealers will correct any mistakes, but good knowledge could save you some grief. Remember, the asking price is not always firm and you may be able to buy for less with some good-natured haggling.

Values of the advertising thimbles are not listed individually. The average value of a plastic advertising thimble is from one to four dollars. The average value of an aluminum advertising thimble is from two to six dollars. Condition and rarity also apply to advertising thimbles.

Abbrevations

GF=Gold Filled   KMD=Ketcham & McDougall
GP=Gold Plated   MOP=Mother of Pearl
HM=Hallmarked   SS=Sterling Silver
HP=Hand Painted   833s=Silver fineness

NPA=no price available

1. USA, SS/Gold band, Stern Bros............$25.00
2. USA, SS/Gold band, Simons..............$25.00
3. USA, GF, Simons.....................$35.00
4. USA, GF, Stern Bros...................$35.00
5. USA, Gold, Quaker type, Brogan........$100.00
6. USA, 14K Gold, Carter, Gough.........$125.00
7. USA, SS/Gold band, Simons.............$40.00
8. USA, SS/Gold band, Stern Bros.........$40.00
9. USA, 10K Gold, KMD.................$100.00
10. Unmarked, Gold....................$50.00
11. German, SS/Gold band, Henckles.........$40.00
12. German, SS/Gold band, Lotthammer-Eber...$40.00
13. Unmarked, Gold paneled................$60.00
14. USA, 10K Gold, KMD.................$300.00
15. Unidentified, Gold scenic.............$80.00
16. Unmarked, 14K Gold Scenic............$100.00
17. USA, 10K Gold paneled, KMD..........$100.00
18. USA, Gold, Modern, Simons...........$100.00
19. USA, Black Hills Gold, SS base.........$50.00
20. Unknown, SS/Gold band...............$20.00
21. USA, SS/Gold band, Goldsmith-Stern......$40.00
22. USA, SS/Gold band, Simons.............$30.00
23. USA, SS/Gold band, KMD..............$45.00
24. USA, 14K Gold, Simons...............$125.00
25. Unmarked, Gold, vintage..............$75.00
26. USA, 10K Gold, Baird-North...........$100.00
27. Unidentified, Gold, "Burr" mark........$60.00
28. Unmarked, Gold....................$50.00
29. USA, 10K Gold, Scenic, Simons.........$125.00
30. USA, SS/Gold band, Simons.............$25.00
31. USA, SS/Gold band, Simons.............$35.00
32. USA, SS/Gold band, Waite-Thresher.......$45.00
33. USA, Gold, Simons.....................$90.00
34. US, SS/Gold band, Simons..............$50.00
35. USA, Gold Overlay, Muhr..............$25.00
36. USA, 10K Gold, Goldsmith-Stern........$100.00
37. USA, GP, Finger Guard, Bradley.........$22.00
38. USA, Gold, Paneled, Barker..............$65.00
39. USA, Gold, Faceted rim, Muhr..........$125.00
40. USA, SS/Gold band, Simons.............$35.00
41. USA, SS/Gold band, Stern Bros..........$35.00
42. USA, 14K Gold/Cameo...................$200.00
43. USA, 14K Gold, Carter, Gough..........$125.00
44. USA, Gold Filled, Stern Bros..........$35.00
45. USA, SS/Gold band, Simons.............$30.00
46. USA, SS/Gold band, Goldsmith-Stern......$30.00
47. USA, Gold, Unidentified................$80.00
48. USA, 10K Gold, Goldsmith-Stern........$85.00
49. USA, 10K Gold, Goldsmith-Stern........$100.00
50. Unidentified, 10K Gold................$100.00
51. USA, 14K Gold, Simons...............$125.00
52. USA, 14K Gold, Simons...............$125.00
53. USA, Gold filled, Stern Bros..........$25.00
54. USA, 14K Gold, Goldsmith-Stern........$125.00
55. USA, 10K Gold, Goldsmith-Stern........$100.00
56. USA, Gold filled, Stern Bros..........$25.00
57. USA, Gold filled, Stern Bros..........$25.00
58. Unmarked, Gold....................$60.00
59. USA, SS/Gold band, Goldsmith-Stern......$40.00
60. USA, SS/Gold band, Simons.............$25.00
61. USA, SS/Gold band, KMD..............$40.00
62. USA, 10K Gold, KMD.................$100.00
63. USA, 10K Gold, Goldsmith-Stern........$100.00
64. USA, 14K Gold, Simons...............$125.00

65. USA, Gold, Brogan.....................$100.00
66. USA, Gold filled, Stern Bros..............$25.00
67. USA, SS/Gold band, Goldsmith-Stern......$40.00
68. USA, SS/Gold band, Simons.............$40.00
69. USA, SS/Gold band, Simons.............$25.00
70. USA, SS/Gold band, Stern Bros...........$55.00
71. USA, SS/Gold band, Brogan.............$40.00
72. USA, SS/Gold band, Muhr..............$40.00
73. USA, SS, Anchors, Waite-Thresher.........$55.00
74. USA, SS, Birds, Stern Bros.............$30.00
75. USA, SS, KMD....................$22.00
76. USA, SS, Fleur de Lis, Brogan...........$25.00
77. USA, SS, Floral, Simons..............$18.00
78. USA, SS, Floral, Goldsmith-Stern.........$15.00
79. USA, SS, Geometric, Simons............$15.00
80. German, SS, Gabler.................$40.00
81. English, SS, Royal Spa, H. Griffith........$55.00
82. USA, SS, Floral, Simons..............$15.00
83. USA, SS, Quaker type, Simons...........$20.00
84. USA, SS, Geometric, Simons............$20.00
85. Portugal, Silver turtle...............$10.00
86. USA, SS, Scenic, Simons.............$45.00
87. English, SF, DORCAS, C. Horner........$40.00
88. USA, SS, Oval shields, Simons..........$20.00
89. USA, SS, Goldsmith-Stern.............$20.00
90. USA, SS, Scenic, Simons.............$35.00
91. USA, SS, Birds, Simons..............$20.00
92. USA, SS, Paneled, Stern Bros...........$20.00
93. USA, SS, Feathers, Stern Bros...........$20.00
94. USA, SS, Feathers, Simons............$22.00
95. USA, SS, Floral, Simons..............$30.00
96. USA, SS, Swags, Stern Bros............$20.00
97. USA, SS, Floral, Simons..............$18.00
98. USA, SS, Fans, Stern Bros............$20.00
99. USA, SS, Scenic, Simons.............$35.00
100. USA, SS, KMD....................$20.00
101. USA, SS, Floral, Simons..............$15.00
102. USA, SS, Right Greek Key, Simons.......$20.00
103. Mexico, Mexico silver..............$20.00
104. English, SS, Hallmark, Swan..........$50.00
105. English, SS, Hallmark, Swan..........$50.00
106. English, SS, Hallmark, Swan..........$50.00
107. English, SS, Hallmark, Swan..........$50.00
108. English, Enamel over SS, HM, Swan......$50.00
109. German, SS/Enamel/Gold inlay, Gabler....$50.00
110. English, SS, Hallmark, Swan..........$50.00
111. USA, SS, Paneled, Goldsmith-Stern.......$20.00
112. Siam, SS, Tai Dancers.............$20.00
113. Unidentified, SS, "JUDD".............$20.00
114. Unidentified, SS, Scenic.............$35.00
115. Mexico, Scenic..................$12.00
116. USA, SS, Flowers, Simons............$20.00
117. USA, SS, Flowers, Waite-Thresher.......$30.00
118. USA, SS, Propeller band, Stern Bros......$20.00
119. USA, SS, Snake & Dot, Simons.........$22.00
120. USA, SS, Asters, Simons.............$20.00
121. USA, SS, Mini-paneled, Simons.........$18.00
122. USA, SS, KMD...................$20.00
123. USA, SS, Full knurling, Stern Bros.......$20.00
124. USA, SS, Scenic, Waite-Thresher........$50.00
125. Italy, 800s, Touchmark.............$25.00
126. English, SF, DORCAS, C. Horner.......$40.00
127. USA, SS, Stern Bros...............$20.00
128. USA, SS, Child's, Simons............$30.00
129. USA, SS, Floral, KMD.............$30.00
130. USA, SS, Raised circles, Stern Bros......$30.00
131. Unmarked, SS, Tailors.............$15.00
132. USA, SS, Ocean wave, Brogan.........$30.00
133. USA, SS, Aiken-Lambert............$50.00
134. USA, SS, Scenic, Waite-Thresher........$45.00
135. USA, SS, Scenic, Brogan............$45.00
136. USA, SS, Paneled, Webster Co.........$30.00

137. Unidentified...................$10.00
138. USA, SS, Priscilla, Simons...........$20.00
139. Unidentified, Buildings.............$20.00
140. USA, SS, Floral, Muhr.............$35.00
141. USA, SS, Floral, Muhr.............$35.00
142. USA, SS, Embroidery, KMD..........$55.00
143. USA, SS, Louis XV edge, KMD.........$35.00
144. USA, SS, Basketweave, Goldsmith-Stern...$18.00
145. USA, SS, Floral, Stern Bros...........$15.00
146. USA, SS, Paneled, Simons...........$15.00
147. Jerusalem, SS, Camel.............$20.00
148. Germany, Enamel/Sterling...........$35.00
149. France, SS, Black Arrow, Lenain........$35.00
150. France, SS, Fleurs et Fruits, Lenain......$35.00
151. USA, SS, Dogwood, Webster.........$42.00
152. Portugal, 925s, Thistle.............$18.00
153. USA, SS, Cherubs, Simons..........$150.00
154. USA, SS, Scroll, Stern Bros...........$30.00
155. USA, SS, Paneled, Webster Co.........$28.00
156. USA, SS, Paneled, Simons...........$28.00
157. Holland, Enamel over Sterling.........$20.00
158. Germany, SS/Enamel/Stone cap........$40.00
159. Germany, SS/Enamel/Stone cap........$40.00
160. Jerusalem, SS, Applied wire..........$20.00
161. France, SS, Wild Rose Bough, Lenain....$35.00
162. France, SS, Dance of Graces, Lenain.....$35.00
163. USA, SS, Snail & Dot, Simons.........$22.00
164. USA, SS, Tiered, Muhr.............$22.00
165. USA, SS, DC Percival by Waite-Thresher..$45.00
166. USA, SS, Simons................$35.00
167. USA, SS, Vintage, Goldsmith-Stern......$45.00
168. USA, SS, Garland, Simons...........$35.00
169. USA, SS, Stern Bros..............$30.00
170. USA, SS, Simons................$30.00
171. USA, SS, Waves, Waite-Thresher.......$20.00
172. USA, SS, Waves, Goldsmith-Stern......$20.00
173. USA, SS, Simons................$18.00
174. USA, SS, Simons................$18.00
175. USA, SS, Faceted rim, KMD..........$20.00
176. USA, SS, Shepard...............$30.00
177. English, SF, DREEMA, H. Griffith......$45.00
178. USA, SS, Rope, Muhr.............$20.00
179. USA, SS, Simons................$15.00
180. Portugal, 833s.................$30.00
181. USA, SS, Diamond knurling, Webster....$40.00
182. USA, SS, "Mother".............$25.00
183. USA, SS, Target band, Simons.........$20.00
184. USA, SS, Simons................$20.00
185. USA, SS, Stitch in Time, Simons.......$200.00
186. USA, SS, Columbian Expo., Simons.....$200.00
187. USA, SS, Arches, Waite-Thresher.......$30.00
188. USA, SS, Scroll, Brogan............$40.00
189. Sweden, SS..................$50.00
190. English, SF, DORCAS, C. Horner.......$40.00
191. English, SF, DORCAS, C. Horner.......$40.00
192. English, SS, Hallmarked, C. Horner......$60.00
193. USA, Pure Coin, Mermod-Jaccard.......$50.00
194. USA, SS, Stern Bros..............$25.00
195. USA, SS, Greek Key, Simons.........$20.00
196. USA, SS, Raised Diamonds, Stern Bros...$30.00
197. USA, SS, KMD.................$25.00
198. France, SS, Lily of Valley, Lenain.......$50.00
199. USA, SS, Muhr................$25.00
200. USA, SS, Waite-Thresher...........$25.00
201. Unidentified, SS................$20.00
202. Mexico, Applied wire work..........$12.00
203. English, HM, Queen Head, Comm.......$50.00
204. USA, SS, Embroidery, Simons.........$50.00
205. English, Silver Cased, Iles..........$18.00
206. Germany, 800s, Lotthammer-Eber......$40.00
207. Germany, SS, Birds & Bees, Gabler.....$50.00
208. USA, SS, Paneled, Simons...........$28.00

209. USA, SS, Simons, members only $45.00
210. English, SS, Zipper, Unmarked $20.00
211. Unidentified, SS $10.00
212. Portugal, Filigree $20.00
213. Portugal, Filigree $20.00
214. Portugal, Silver plated $18.00
215. USA, SS, Repro. Salem Witch $25.00
216. English, Child's $15.00
217. USA, SS, Embroidery, Waite-Thresher $50.00
218. USA, SS, Simons $35.00
219. USA, SS, Christmas 1982 . . . . $45.00
220. USA, SS, Stern Bros. $20.00
221. UK, SS, Hallmark Cards $15.00
222. USA, SS, Stern Bros $25.00
223. USA, SS, Diamond knurling, KMD $35.00
224. USA, SS, KMD $35.00
225. Italy, 800s $15.00
226. English, Enamel over Sterling, Swan $45.00
227. English, SS, Hallmarked, Swan $45.00
228. USA, SS, Flowers, Brogan $25.00
229. USA, SS, Left Greek Key, Goldsmith-Stern $25.00
230. USA, SS, Stern Bros. $20.00
231. USA, SS, Simons $18.00
232. Unidentified, SS, Buildings $40.00
233. Israel, SS, Filigree $30.00
234. English, Enamel over Sterling, Swan $50.00
235. USA, SS, Souvenir, Simons $35.00
236. English, SS, Hallmark, Swan $50.00
237. USA, SS, Towle $30.00
238. USA, SS, Simons $35.00
239. USA, SS, Diamond knurling, KMD $35.00
240. Jerusalem, SS $25.00
241. Italy, 800s/Stones $25.00
242. Italy, 800s $25.00
243. Portugal, 925s $12.00
244. France, SS, Red Riding Hood, Lenain $35.00
245. USA, SS Pierced, Brand $20.00
246. USA, SS, Pierced, Brand $28.00
247. USA, SS, Paneled, Muhr $35.00
248. Germany, SS, Leaf border $30.00
249. Germany, SS, Gabler $30.00
250. USA, SS, Tailors, Goldsmith-Stern $20.00
251. English, SF, DORCAS, C. Horner $45.00
252. Germany, SS/Stone top, 925s $40.00
253. USA, SS, Paneled, Stern Bros. $20.00
254. Unidentified, SS, Buildings, Lamson $20.00
255. Illegible, SS $15.00
256. English, SS, Hallmarked, Swan $35.00
257. Unidentified, SS, Beading $15.00
258. Portugal, SS, 925s $20.00
259. USA, SS, Tailors, Goldsmith-Stern $20.00
260. USA, SS, Scrolls, Brogan $35.00
261. USA, SS, Muhr $40.00
262. English, SS, Hallmarked, Fenton $50.00
263. USA, SS, Stern Bros. $30.00
264. USA, SS, Applied roses, Waite-Thresher . . $45.00
265. USA, SS, Paneled, Simons $20.00
266. USA, SS, Ovals, Simons $30.00
267. Unidentified, SS, Advertising $40.00
268. USA, SS, Simons $22.00
269. USA, SS, Floral, Simons $25.00
270. USA, SS, Brogan $30.00
271. English, SS, Hallmarked, Griffith $75.00
272. USA, SS, Louis XV edge, Simons $45.00
273. USA, SS, Bass $50.00
274. USA, SS, Scenic, Muhr $45.00
275. USA, SS, Simons $20.00
276. Israel, 925s, Limited Ed. Yaacov Yemin . . . $45.00
277. USA, SS, Paneled, Muhr $35.00
278. USA, SS, Muhr $35.00
279. USA, SS, Raised Diamonds, Stern Bros. . . . $35.00
280. Sweden, 830s $30.00

281. Germany, SS, Beaded, Gabler $30.00
282. USA, SS, Birds, Brogan $40.00
283. Germany, SS/Stone cap $30.00
284. England, SS, Hallmark, Walker $55.00
285. USA, SS, Simons $30.00
286. USA, SS, Webster $30.00
287. England, SS, Hallmarked, Griffith $65.00
288. USA, SS, Houses, Simons $35.00
289. Unidentified, SS, Mt. Vernon $30.00
290. England, SS, Hallmarked, S. Bros. $80.00
291. England, SS, Hallmarked, HW Ltd. $75.00
292. USA, SS, Floral, KMD $40.00
293. Germany, SS, Floral $40.00
294. USA, SS, Good Luck, Stern Bros. $35.00
295. Germany, SS, Drapes, Gabler $40.00
296. English, SS, Hallmarked, Rose $35.00
297. USA, SS, Diamond knurling, Webster $30.00
298. USA, SS, Stern Bros. $20.00
299. USA, SS, KMD $40.00
300. England, Silver Cased, Iles $40.00
301. USA, SS, Stern Bros. $20.00
302. USA, SS, Simons $25.00
303. USA, SS, Columbian Expo., Simons $200.00
304. USA, SS, "Golden Spike", Simons $200.00
305. USA, SS, Cherubs, KMD $160.00
306. USA, SS, Scenic, Simons $45.00
307. USA, SS, Waite-Thresher $25.00
308. Germany, SS $25.00
309. USA, SS, Brogan $25.00
310. USA, SS, Simons $20.00
311. USA, SS, KMD $25.00
312. English, Silver Filled, DORCAS $40.00
313. English, SS, THE SPA, HM, Griffith $35.00
314. USA, SS, Shepard $35.00
315. USA, SS, Paneled, Brogan $35.00
316. USA, SS, Scenic, Waite-Thresher $50.00
317. USA, SS, Stern Bros. $30.00
318. German, SS/Stone cap $30.00
319. USA, SS, Scenic, Stern Bros. $50.00
320. USA, SS, Floral, Waite-Thresher $40.00
321. USA, SS, Vintage, Simons $50.00
322. USA, SS, Cherubs, Simons $50.00
323. Unidentified, SS $25.00
324. USA, SS, Simons $20.00
325. USA, SS, Paneled, Waite-Thresher $30.00
326. USA, SS, Flowers, Stern Bros. $25.00
327. USA, SS, Leaf, Brogan $30.00
328. USA, SS, Paneled, Stern Bros. $20.00
329. USA, SS, Links, Brogan $20.00
330. USA, SS, Stern Bros. $20.00
331. Unidentified, SS, Hand punched $18.00
332. Portugal, 925s $20.00
333. Portugal, 925s $28.00
334. Mexico, 925s $20.00
335. Germany, 925s, Greif $40.00
336. Germany, 925s, Prandl $40.00
337. Unknown, Brass $6.00
338. England, HER MAJESTY $18.00
339. Unmarked, Brass $6.00
340. Unmarked, Brass, Greek Key $6.00
341. England, Brass, Leaf & Berry $6.00
342. Unmarked, Brass, Threader/cutter $10.00
343. Unmarked, Brass, Applied grape design . . . $6.00
344. Unmarked, Brass, Applied Butterfly $6.00
345. Unmarked, Fluted band, Brass $5.00
346. Germany, Brass, tiered $4.00
347. Unmarked, Brass, Tiered $4.00
348. Unmarked, Brass, Fluted $5.00
349. Unmarked, Brass, Tailors $12.00
350. China, Unmarked, Brass, Ring type $3.00
351. USA, Unmarked, Brass, Prudential $8.00
352. USA, Brass, Prudential $8.00

353. Austria, Brass.........................$6.00
354. Austria, Brass, Peti-point band...........$6.00
355, 356. USA, King Features..............ea $5.00
357-360. USA, Walt Disney................ea $5.00
361. Unmarked, Brass......................$4.00
362. USA, Brass, Brand....................$20.00
363. Unmarked, Brass......................$6.00
364. Unmarked, Brass......................$8.00
365. Unmarked, Brass......................$8.00
366. Unmarked, Brass, Tailors.............$12.00
367. USA, Brass, Magic Thimble...........$12.00
368. England, Brass......................$6.00
369. Germany, Brass.......................$6.00
370. Austria, Brass.......................$10.00
371. Austria, Brass.......................$10.00
372. Brass Monopoly Game Piece (1985)........NPA
373. Austria, Brass.......................$6.00
374. Austria, Collector Circle Member..........$4.00
375. Germany, Brass.......................$6.00
376. Unmarked, Brass......................$6.00
377. England, Brass, Iles................$45.00
378. Unmarked, Brass......................$8.00
379. Unmarked, Child's brass...............$4.00
380. Unmarked, Brass, Cutter..............$5.00
381. Unmarked, Brass......................$6.00
382. Germany, Brass......................$10.00
383. Austria, Brass......................$10.00
384. Unmarked, Brass.....................$10.00
385. Unmarked, Brass, Engraved...........$20.00
386. Germany, Brass.......................$8.00
387. Unmarked, Brass, Child's.............$8.00
388. Germany, Brass......................$10.00
389. English, Brass, Child's.............$10.00
390. England, Brass.....................$10.00
391. Unmarked, Brass....................$10.00
392. Unmarked, Brass....................$15.00
393. Austria, Brass.......................$6.00
394. Unmarked, Brass, "REGARD"............$8.00
395. Unmarked, Brass....................$15.00
396. Nepal, Brass, Applied wire...........$5.00
397. Holland, Brass, China cap............$6.00
398. USA, Silver Dollar City.............$10.00
399. Holland, Brass, China cap............$6.00
400. Unmarked, Brass....................$12.00
401. German, Brass, Gabler..............$35.00
402. Unmarked, Brass......................$6.00
403. Unmarked, Brass.....................$10.00
404. Unmarked, Brass......................$8.00
405. Unmarked, Brass, Bronze finish..........$6.00
406. Austria, Brass......................$10.00
407. Unmarked, Brass......................$6.00
408. Unmarked, Brass......................$8.00
409-411. Zimbabwe, Africa, Ivory..........NPA
412. Unmarked, Ivory....................$15.00
413. Unmarked, Ivory....................$15.00
414. India, White Camel Bone............$10.00
415. India, White Camel Bone............$10.00
416. Paraguay, Genuine Horn.............$17.00
417-419. English "Peeps", Woodsetton.....$15.00
420. USA, Pewter, Gish..................$13.00
421. USA, Pewter, Gish..................$14.00
422. Unidentified, Pewter................$8.00
423. USA, Pewter, Gish..................$12.00
424. USA, Unmarked......................$6.00
425. English "peep", Woodsetton.........$15.00
426. Unmarked, Pewter, Collector Circle Member.$4.00
427. Unmarked, Pewter, For a Good Girl......$10.00
428. Unmarked, Pewter, Charm.............$3.00
429. England, Pewter, Scenic, Battersea......$20.00
430. USA, Pewter, Train, Coronodo........$12.00
431. USA, Pewter, Gish..................$14.00
432. Unmarked, Pewter, Souvenir...........$4.00

433. USA, Pewter, Gish..................$12.00
434. Unmarked, Pewter, Souvenir..........$6.00
435. Unmarked, Pewter, Souvenir..........$6.00
436. Unmarked, Pewter, Souvenir..........$5.00
437. Holland, Pewter, China cap.........$10.00
438. Unmarked, Pewter, Souvenir..........$5.00
439. Unmarked, Pewter, Souvenir..........$5.00
440. USA, Pewter, Six Flags, Gish.......$10.00
441. Unmarked, Pewter, Souvenir..........$5.00
442. Unidentified, China, Touchmarked......$4.00
443. Unmarked, China, Souvenir...........$4.00
444. USA, China, Personalized...........$10.00
445. Unmarked, China, Roses............$10.00
446. Unmarked, China, Blue Delft.........$4.00
447. France, Limoges.....................$4.00
448. USA, China, Belmar.................$8.00
449. Germany, China, Souvenir............$6.00
450. England, China......................$5.00
451. England, Bone China, Ashleydale......$10.00
452. Germany, China, Limited Ed. Meissen....$130.00
453. USA, China/Pewter, Heirloom Ed........$9.00
454. England, Bone China.................$6.00
455. England, Bone China, Theodore Paul.....$6.00
456. England, Jasperware, Wedgewood......$26.00
457. England, Jasperware, Wedgewood......$25.00
458. England, Bone China, Wedgewood........$8.00
459. Italy, China, Barsato..............$17.00
460. England, China, Spode.............$10.00
461. England, Pottery, Lord Nelson........$5.00
462. England, China, Ansley............$14.00
463. USA, China, HP, Betty Daley.........$5.00
464. England, China, Caverswall.........$12.00
465. Germany, China, Bareuther...........$8.00
466. Japan, China......................$15.00
467. England, China, Royal Worcester......$15.00
468. Spain, Unglazed Porcelain, Llardo'....$15.00
469. France, China, Haviland...........$15.00
470. USA, Franciscian...................$15.00
471. Japan, Bone China, Noritake.........$15.00
472. England, China, Spode.............$15.00
473. Germany, China, Hutschenreuther.....$15.00
474. Italy, China, Ginori...............$15.00
475. The Netherlands, China, Mosa........$15.00
476. Ireland, China, Royal Tara.........$15.00
477. England, Jasperware, Wedgewood......$15.00
478. France, China, Bernardaud..........$15.00
479. England, China, Adams.............$15.00
480. Japan, China, Okura...............$15.00
481. England, China, Crown Staffs.......$15.00
482. England, Ironstone, Johnson Bros.....$15.00
483. England, China, Coalport..........$15.00
484. USA, China, Franklin Porcelain......$15.00
485. England, China, Masons............$15.00
486. Denmark, China, Royal Copenhagen....$15.00
487. England, Bone China, Royal Adderley....$15.00
488. Sweden, China, Rorstrand..........$15.00
489. England, Bone China, Hammersley.....$15.00
490. England, Bone China, Royal Albert....$15.00
491. England, Bone China, Royal Doulton....$15.00
492. USA, Ceramic, I. Sanchez...........$5.00
493. Unmarked, Ironstone................$3.00
494. Japan, China, Rockwell...........$10.00
495. Japan, China, Rockwell...........$10.00
496-501. USA, Rockwell, Gorham.........ea $15.00
502-507. USA, Advertising, Franklin Porc....ea $15.00
508-550. USA, First Ladies, Franklin Porc....ea $15.00
551-554. USA, Alum., Whistle Thimbles, B&B.ea $15.00
555-569. USA, Plastic Advertising.......ea $1.00-4.00
570-590. Aluminum Advertising.........ea $2.00-6.00
591. Unmarked, Base Metal Adv. Ideal.......$5.00
592. USA, Brass, Prudential.............$8.00
593. Unmarked, SS, Advertising.........$40.00

594. Unmarked, SS Advertising $15.00
595. England, SS, Advertising, Walker $55.00
596. Unmarked, Base Metal $5.00
597. Unmarked, Copper $3.00
598. Germany, Base Metal $2.00
599. Unmarked, Base Metal, Cutter $1.00
600. USA, Cutter/Threader $10.00
601. England, Base Metal $4.00
602-605. Unmarked, Star on cap . . . . ea $2.00
606-608. USA, Simons Industrial . . . . ea $6.00
609. Unmarked, Tailors $5.00
610. Unmarked, Steel Tailor $3.00
611. Germany, Steel/brass lined, Tailor $5.00
612. Unmarked, Steel Tailor $5.00
613-615. Mexico, Abalone/Brass . . . . ea $8.00
616. Unmarked, Metal Child's $2.00
617. USA, Wooden, Mathis . . . . NPA
618. USA, Wooden, HP $2.00
619. USA, Aspen Wood $3.00
620. USA, Crocheted, Mathis $5.00
621-623. England, Metal . . . . ea $2.00
624. Spain, Metal $1.00
625-629. Poland, Metal . . . . ea $1.00-3.00
630. Unmarked, Metal, Tailor $4.00
631. Unmarked, Steel, Tailor $4.00
632. USA, Leather $3.00
633. Unmarked, Steel/Brass lined $3.00
634. Unmarked, Pewter, For a Good Girl $10.00
635. England, Metal, Iles $6.00
636. USA, Alloy, Charms $5.00
637. England, Metal $6.00
638. USA, Metal, Cutter $8.00
639-640. Unmarked, Cloisonne . . . . ea $6.00
641. USA, Bronze, Fort, Collector Circle Member . $4.00
642. Germany, Metal $1.00
643-644. Aluminum, Brass lined . . . . ea $2.00
645. England, Steel, Tailor $3.00
646. Unmarked, Aluminum $1.00
647. USA, Copper, Mathis $20.00
648. India, Teak Wood $10.00
649. USA, Oak Wood, HP, signed, dated $5.00
650. Jerusalem, Olive Wood . . . . NPA
652. Italy, Wood, Anri $10.00
653. West Germany, Leaded Glass $9.00
654. Italy, Glass, Mary Gregory type $18.00
655. USA, Glass, Etched $8.00
656. USA, Glass, Etched, Scalloped $10.00
657. Unmarked, Glass, Painted $8.00
658. USA, Plastic, Adjustable $2.00
659. USA, Plastic finger guard $1.00
660. USA, Metal/Brass, Needle guard $4.00
661. Unmarked, Cutter/Threader $2.00
662. England, Metal, Iles $12.00
663. Unmarked, Aluminum, Two tier $1.00
664. USA, Alloy, Simons Industrial $4.00
665. Unmarked, Plastic, Magnet top $2.00
666. Unmarked, Brass, Bluebells $9.00
667. USA, Alloy, Simons Industrial $8.00
668-669. Austria, Mother-Daughter set $8.00
670. Unmarked, Metal/Cutter $8.00
671. USA, Metal, Mother & Child $4.00
672. USA, Coal $5.00
673. Austria, Aluminum/Stone top $4.00
674. Unmarked, Aluminum $1.00
675. Unmarked, Aluminum $1.00
676-681. Unmarked, Aluminum Quilters nest . set $8.00
682-683. Unmarked, Aluminum . . . . ea $1.00-3.00
684. Unmarked, Glass $10.00
685. Unmarked, Glass $8.00
686. Italy, Millefiori Glass $10.00
687. Unmarked, Alabaster $10.00
688. Italy, Murano Glass $10.00

689. Unmarked, Glass $12.00
690. USA, Quilters Leather Guard $2.00
691. England, Rubber finger stall $2.00
692. USA, Quilters Leather Guard $2.00
693. Unmarked, Sailor's Palm $30.00
694. Germany, Thimble/Bee's wax holder $85.00
695. England, Thread case, SS $125.00
696. Unmarked, Walnut Thimble Case $45.00
697-698. England, Embossed cases . . . . ea $45.00
699. Unmarked, Leather thimble case $40.00
700. Unmarked, Wicker basket $2.00
701. USA, SS/Gold, Thimble holder, Tiffany . . . $200.00
702. Russian, SS, Thimble holder $175.00
703. USA, SS/Gold Thimble holder, Unger $150.00
704. Unmarked, SS, Thimble holder $150.00
705. England, SS, Thimble holder $200.00
706. USA, SS/Plush holder, Tiffany $200.00
707. USA, SS/Gold plated holder, Tiffany $200.00
708. USA, SS, Thimble holder, Unger $125.00
709. Unmarked, Presentation box . . . . NPA
710. USA, SS/GP, Thimble holder, Foster & Bailey $150.00
711. India, Brass/Applied wire, holder $10.00
712. China, Cloisonne holder $15.00
713. Unmarked, MOP thimble holder $35.00
714. USA, SS, Thimble holder, Webster $125.00
715. USA, SS, Thimble holder, Webster $125.00
716. USA, SS, Thimble holder, Gorham $150.00
717. USA, SP, Thimble holder, Silvermans $30.00
718. Unmarked, Sweet grass holder $14.00
719. Unmarked, SS, Holder & Thimble $250.00
720. Unmarked, Vegetable Ivory set $85.00
721. Unmarked, Vegetable Ivory set $100.00
722. Unmarked, Vegetable Ivory set $85.00
723. Unmarked, MOP Holder . . . . NPA
724. Unmarked, Presentation case, casket type . . . NPA
725. Unmarked, Presentation case, casket type . . . NPA
726. Unmarked, plush lined presentation case . . . . NPA
727. Unmarked, Satin lined presentation case . . . . NPA
728. England, Holder for Iles thimble . . . . NPA
729. Germany, China, Holder & Thimble $12.00
730. Unmarked, China, Holder & Thimble $10.00
731. England, China, Needle case & Thimble . . . $12.00
732. Unmarked, WW I Sewing kit $8.00
733. Unmarked, WW II Sewing kit $5.00
734. Unmarked, Suede sewing kit $5.00
735. Unmarked, Coca-Cola mending kit $4.00
736. USA, Political mending kit $2.00
737. Unmarked, Lydia Pinkham case $10.00
738. Germany, Brass/enameled mending kit $5.00
739. Unmarked, Plastic mending kit $2.00
740. Unmarked, Lydia Pinkham mending kit $8.00
741. Germany, Advertising kit $6.00
742. Unmarked, Celluloid mending kit $5.00
743. Germany, Celluloid mending kit $4.00
744. Unmarked, Plastic Doll mending kit $3.00
745. Germany, Lighter type mending kit $10.00
746. Austria, Plated brass kit $5.00
747. Germany, Embossed metal kit $4.00
748. Austria, Gilded brass/Needlepoint kit $8.00
749. Unmarked, Folding/Ivory fittings $15.00
750. French, SS, Matched sewing set $125.00
751. French, SS, Matched set, P. Lenain $125.00
752. French, SS $100.00
753. English, SS, Pin Cushion, D&LS $45.00
754. USA, SP, Thread spool holder $20.00
755. Unmarked, SS, Strawberry emery $20.00
756. Unmarked, SS, Tape measure $15.00
757. Unmarked, Vegetable Ivory needle case $30.00
758. Unmarked, Ivory needle case $20.00
759. Unmarked, Ivory stiletto $15.00
760. Unmarked, SS, Measure gauge $35.00
761. Unmarked, SS, Needle case $50.00

762. Unmarked, Ivory Thread winder.........$10.00
763. USA, SS, Tatting Shuttle, Nussbaum & Hunold $35.00
764. Unmarked, SS handle darner............$50.00
765. Unmarked, SS adjustable stiletto......$35.00
766. USA, China, Thimble servant, Schmid....$15.00
767. Unmarked, Metal, Sewing stand.........$30.00
768. Unmarked, Wooden sewing box..........$75.00
769. Unmarked, Plush sewing box............$50.00
770. Unmarked, Silk Chatelaine.............$25.00
771. USA, Clark's sewing box, Tollner........$35.00
772. Unmarked, Sewing bird.................$125.00
773. Unmarked, Ivory clamp pin cushion......$50.00
774. Unmarked, Cast iron clamp.............$25.00
775. USA, SS, Glove darner, Webster.........$45.00
776. Unmarked, SS, Glove darner............$45.00
777. Unmarked, Brass needle holder...........$9.00
778. Italy, Brass scissor....................$5.00

779. Germany, Steel, scissor.................$12.00
780. Unmarked, Brass scissor.................$8.00
781. Unmarked, Goat cart thimble holder......$35.00
782-783. USA, Hallmark Angels.............ea $8.00
784. Unmarked, Glass holder.................$15.00
785. Unmarked, China shoe holder............$10.00
786. Unmarked, China thimble holder.........$10.00
787. Unmarked, Pewter thimble stand.........$20.00
788. Unmarked, Pewter thimble stand.........$12.00
789. Austria, Bronze rooster, thimble stand....$20.00
790. Unmarked, Wooden doll thimble & case....$12.00
791. Unmarked, Cast/Gilded Thread holder....$65.00
792. Germany, Stickware mending egg.........$20.00
793. Unmarked, Wooden darner................$5.00
794. Unmarked, Glass holder.................$6.00
795. USA, SS, Jigger, Thomae...............$50.00

Selected Reading:

Greif, Helmut. *Talks About Thimbles*, 1984

Holmes, E.F. *Thimbles*, 1976

_____. *A History of Thimbles*, 1985

Johnson, Eleanor. *Thimbles*, Shire Album #96, 1982

_____. *Needlework Tools*, Shire Album #38, 1978

Lundquist, Myrtle. *The Book of 1000 Thimbles*, 1970

_____. *Thimble Treasury*, 1975

_____. *Thimble Americana*, 1981

Philadelphia Thimble Society, *Henry Muhr and Sons*, 1985

Rainwater, D.T. *Encyclopedia of American Silver Manufacturers*, 1975

Rath, J.A. *Antique and Unusual Thimbles*, 1979

Rogers, G.A. *Needlework Tools*, 1983

von Hoelle, J.J. *Thimble Collector's Encyclopedia*, 1983

_____. *The Family Simons*, 1985

_____. *The Story of Stern Brothers & Co.*, 1985

Whiting, Gertrude. *Tools and Toys of Stitchery*, 1928

Wyler, S.B. *Book of Old Silver*, 1937

Periodicals:

Thimbleletter, Published six times a year by Lorraine M. Crosby, 93 Walnut Hill Rd., Newton Highlands, Mass. 02161

T.C.I. Bulletin, Published quarterly by Thimble Collectors International for members. Inquiries to Idabelle Forker, P.O. Box 2311, Des Moines, Iowa 50310

Two Important Tools For The
Astute Antique Dealer, Collector and Investor

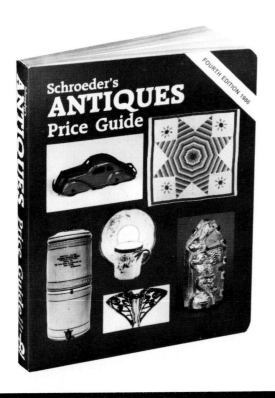

Schroeder's Antiques Price Guide

The very best low cost investment that you can make if you are really serious about antiques and collectibles is a good identification and price guide. We publish and highly recommend **Schroeder's Antiques Price Guide**. Our editors and writers are very careful to seek out and report accurate values each year. We do not simply change the values of the items each year but start anew to bring you an entirely new edition. If there are repeats, they are by chance and not by choice. Each huge edition (it weighs 3 pounds!) has over 50,000 descriptions and current values on 608 - 8½x11 pages. There are hundreds and hundreds of categories and even more illustrations. Each topic is introduced by an interesting discussion that is an education in itself. Again, no dealer, collector or investor can afford not to own this book. It is available from your favorite bookseller or antiques dealer at the low price of $11.95. If you are unable to find this price guide in your area, it's available from Collector Books, P.O. Box 3009, Paducah, KY 42001 at $11.95 plus $1.00 for postage and handling.

Flea Market Trader

Bargains are pretty hard to come by these days -- especially in the field of antiques and collectibles, and everyone knows that the most promising sources for those seldom-found under-priced treasures are flea markets. To help you recognize a bargain when you find it, you'll want a copy of the *Flea Market Trader*--the only price guide on the market that deals exclusively with all types of merchandise you'll be likely to encounter in the marketplace. It contains not only reliable pricing information, but the *Flea Market Trader* will be the first to tune you in to the market's newest collectible interests -- you will be able to buy before the market becomes established, before prices have a chance to escalate! You'll not only have the satisfaction of being first in the know, but you'll see your investments appreciate dramatically. You will love the format. Its handy 5½"x8½" size will tuck easily into pocket or purse. Its common sense organization along with detailed index makes finding your subject a breeze. There's tons of information and hundreds of photos to aid in identification. It's written with first-hand insight and an understanding of market activities. It's reliable, informative, comprehensive; it's a bargain! From Collector Books, P.O. Box 3009 Paducah, Kentucky 42001. $8.95 plus $1.00 postage and handling.

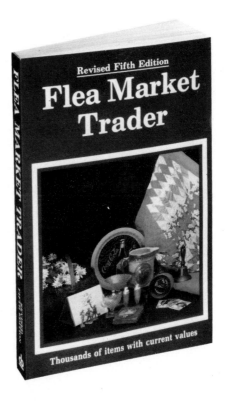